SEEKERS, SAINTS, AND SINNERS

SEEKERS, SAINTS, AND SINNERS

LIFE-CHANGING ENCOUNTERS WITH JESUS

H. STEPHEN SHOEMAKER

JUDSON PRESS
PUBLISHERS SINCE 1824
VALLEY FORGE, PA

Judson Press has made every effort to trace the ownership of all quotes. In the event of a question arising from the use of a quote, we regret any error made and will be pleased to make the necessary correction in future printings and editions of this book.

Unless otherwise noted, Bible quotations in this volume are from the New Revised Standard Version of the Bible, copyright © 1989 by the Division of Christian Education of the National Council of the Churches of Christ in the United States of America. Used by permission. All rights reserved.

Scripture quotations marked KJV are from *The Holy Bible*, King James Version.

Scripture quotations marked NIV are from the Holy Bible, New International Version®, NIV®. Copyright © 1973, 1978, 1984, 2011 by Biblica, Inc.™ Used by permission of Zondervan. All rights reserved worldwide. www.zondervan.com. The "NIV"and "New International Version" are trademarks registered in the United States Patent and Trademark Office by Biblica, Inc.™

Scripture quotations marked RSV are from the Revised Standard Version of the Bible, copyright © 1946, 1952, 1971 by the Division of Christian Educa-tion of the National Council of the Churches of Christ in the U.S.A. Used by permission.

Interior design by Beth Oberholtzer.
Cover design by David Shoemaker.

Library of Congress Cataloging-in-Publication data

Cataloging-in-Publication Data available upon request. Contact cip@judson press.com.

Printed in the U.S.A.

First printing, 2019.

*To Sue
and to Grace Baptist Church*

Contents

Acknowledgments

No book is written without a company of friends and helpers. I wish to thank Rebecca Irwin-Diehl, editor of Judson Press, and the professional staff at Judson Press for their collaboration in this project. Judson Press is an important arm in the ministry of American Baptist Churches USA, and I am grateful for our "partnership in the gospel" (Philippians 1:5, NIV). I thank again Amy Jones, masterful preparer of this manuscript.

I wish to thank Grace Baptist Church, Statesville, North Carolina, which has become my community of faith as I have served them first as interim pastor and now as pastor. They heard some of these chapters first in the form of sermons. And I wish to thank Sue, my new partner in marriage and ministry, a grace indeed. Hence my dedication to both Sue and Grace Baptist Church. The gospel is lived out in relationship.

Introduction

It has been said that the shortest distance between two people is a story. Let me tell you a story, eleven stories actually, in ten chapters. These are stories about encounters with Jesus in the New Testament Gospels.

The title of this book is *Seekers, Saints, and Sinners*. Jesus received all who came to him: rich, poor, sick and well; women, men, and young children; Jew, Samaritan, and Gentile. He ate with tax collectors *and* Pharisees, seekers, sinners, and saints in the making. He not only received them, he went out to them, like a shepherd going after a lost sheep. As he said to Zacchaeus: "The Son of Man came to seek and to save the lost" (Luke 19:10). There are so many ways to be lost—lost in doubt and lost in one's certainty, lost in sin and lost in one's righteousness, lost in hopelessness, loneliness and confusion, lost far from home and lost close to home. Jesus sought them all, us all.

One cannot understand the ministry of Jesus apart from his relationships, both ongoing relationships and onetime encounters. This book focuses on onetime encounters with Jesus. We may meet not only Jesus there but ourselves in the miracle of recognition.

Jewish philosopher Martin Buber wrote in his classic work *I and Thou*, "All real living is meeting. . . . In the beginning is relation."[1] The Bible is full of meetings with God—and the consequences of those meetings. Abraham met God in a call to leave his homeland and move toward a promised land and to become a people of God's promise. Moses met God in a burning bush and received a call to free the Hebrew people from slavery in Egypt. Isaiah met God, high and lifted up, in the temple and was called to be a prophet to God's people. Ruth met the God of *hesed*—steadfast love—in her relationship with her mother-in-law, Naomi, and was called to embody God's *hesed* in her new village of Bethlehem. Amos, a sheepherder, met God when he was with his flock and was enlisted to be a prophet to Israel. Ezekiel met God in visions and prophesied for God. And people in the Gospels met God in Jesus, in relationship and encounters. All were changed in the meeting. "All real living is meeting. . . . In the beginning is relation."

I offer these eleven stories as opportunities to meet ourselves and to meet Jesus. Celtic Christians speak of "thin places" where the veil between earth and heaven, the material and the spiritual, grows transparent and we can glimpse God. These stories have been "thin places" and meeting places for me. I hope they will be so for you.

Chapter 1 explores Jesus' encounter with Nicodemus (John 3:1-12). We will learn, along with Nicodemus, about the mystery of new birth. We will explore the meanings of "new birth" and the manifold ways the Spirit births us into new life. There is more than one way to experience conversion.

In chapter 2 we will delve into Jesus' encounter with the Samaritan woman and the "living water" Jesus offers (John 4:1-42). He crosses the boundaries of race, gender, religion, and nationality to bring her eternal life. What boundaries do we need to cross in order to bring people the love of God?

We will meet the paralyzed man at the pool of Bethesda (John 5:1-9) in chapter 3 and consider Jesus' question, "Wilt thou be made whole?" (verse 6, KJV). I will explore the isolation of this man and the healing initiative of Jesus. Whom will we help to get into the pool of healing waters? And, how have we experienced healing in our lives?

Chapter 4 highlights the dialogue between Jesus and the Canaanite woman in Matthew 15:21-28. Her verbal jousting with Jesus appears to have changed his mind about healing her daughter. That same verbal sparring may have changed his mind about the reach of his mission: going beyond the "lost sheep of the house of Israel" (Matthew 10:6, KJV) to lost people everywhere.

In chapter 5 we witness the encounter between Jesus, the woman "taken" in adultery (John 8:3), and her accusers (John 8:1-10). This "orphan text" floated around in the era of the Gospels' writing. The church would not let it go because it said something crucial about Jesus. In chapter 8, John gave it a place in his Gospel.

In Chapter 6 we will consider the story of the "bent-over" woman (Luke 13:10-17). Jesus released her from her eighteen-year-long infirmity. I will join her story with two others: Frederick Buechner's story of the dungeon called "Little Ease" and a most personal story of my own.

Chapter 7 explores two encounters of Jesus that focus on a person's relationship with money and possessions: the accounts of the "rich young ruler" (Mark 10:17-27) and of Zacchaeus (Luke 19:1-10). In the first account the "rich young ruler" said no to Jesus' invitation to sell all, give the money to the poor, and come follow him. He went sadly away. In the second account, Zacchaeus, in response to the divine friendship offered by Jesus, dramatically altered his life and his relationship with wealth. In Jesus' life, some said yes and some said no.

In chapter 8 we'll see that Jesus' healing of a blind man took two tries! That encounter will help us ponder healing as a journey toward wholeness (Mark 8:22-26). Sometimes salvation, healing, and wholeness take time, so don't lose hope!

Chapter 9 will engage us in an investigation of the healing of a blind man named Bartimaeus (Mark 10:46-52). This account contains the heart of the church's evangelical ministry: "Take heart; get up, he is calling you" (verse 49). And it offers the crucial question of Jesus to Bartimaeus and to us: "What do you want me to do for you?" (verse 51). Is not the glad heart of true evangelism helping people get to Jesus and helping them hear his voice? How would you or your church answer if Jesus asked you the simple and disarming question: "What do you want me to do for you?"

In chapter 10 we will discover a woman of Bethany, unnamed in Mark, entering a room where Jesus was dining and anointing his head with costly perfumed oil (Mark 14:3-9). Some of the disciples objected to this lavish display of love, as they noted that the money could have been used to feed the poor. But Jesus received it, for there is always room for extravagant devotion and this was a time for extravagance.

The stories in this book operate as a Venn diagram:

Where the stories overlap, the possibility of transformation exists. The Spirit is present; the kingdom of God that Jesus preached has drawn near, as near as your own breath, as near as your God-seeking heart.

NOTES

1. Martin Buber, *I and Thou* (New York: Scribner, 1958), 11, 18.

Chapter 1

JESUS AND Nicodemus

The Mystery of New Birth
(John 3:1-12)

In the encounter between Jesus and Nicodemus in John 3, Jesus offers us the mystery of new birth.

"Born again" is Jesus' term, and it is used by American evangelical Christians. I can see and hear Billy Graham at his crusades, with his piercing eyes and commanding voice, repeat Jesus' words to Nicodemus: "You must be born again." We see it scrawled on roadside signs: "You must be born again."

Some people divide the Christian world into the "born again," or "real" Christians, and all the rest whose salvation is suspect. This is regrettable. Such use of the phrase makes the phrase itself suspect. It is another dreary example of the human desire to make oneself or one's religion "separate and superior."[1]

When Jimmy Carter, a Southern Baptist, was running for president, he identified himself as a "born-again Christian." It made a lot of people, especially outside of the South, nervous—as if born-again Christians were a cultic or superior form of Christianity.

We make mistakes when we try to make all Christian religious experience the same and force certain forms of

Christian experience on everybody. Consider the case of famous nineteenth-century poet Emily Dickinson, for example. When the Great Awakening revival swept across New England and through Dickinson's hometown, she was the only one in her family and one of the few in her town who refused to be converted in the way everyone was being converted. She never had a "conversion experience" by the conventional definition. That took no small measure of courage and integrity. Her letters poignantly reveal that she wanted to experience what the others were experiencing, but she didn't and wouldn't fake a conversion.[2] The formula for conversion at that time didn't fit her spiritual life. Her love for God seemed always with her. She experienced God everywhere. As she wrote to a dear friend, "This is but Earth, yet Earth so like to heaven, that I would hesitate, should the true one call me away."[3]

"Born again" is a powerful image of Christian faith, but we should not narrow it into one kind of experience—no two births are exactly alike. The new birth is a mystery that Jesus explored in his encounter with Nicodemus. A God without mystery is an idol. We reduce God to fit inside our human imagination; God becomes an idol of the mind. God is greater than our minds can grasp.

The Initial Conversation

Nicodemus was a "leader of the Jews," a position of religious and social standing. He had a lot to lose. He came to Jesus not in broad daylight but under the cover of night. He did not want to be seen with Jesus—not yet—for that would expose him to the sharp disapproval of his religious circle. But Jesus received him exactly as he came, as he receives all seekers of every kind.

Nicodemus was attracted to Jesus because Jesus had something Nicodemus wanted. Yet he felt threatened by Jesus, for Jesus placed a question mark at the center of Nicodemus's religiosity.

Nicodemus came to Jesus and said:

"Rabbi, we know that you are a teacher who has come from God; for no one can do these signs that you do apart from the presence of God." (3:2)

Jesus wasted no time getting to the heart of things:

"Very truly, I tell you, no one can see the kingdom of God without being born from above [born again]." (3:3)

Although Jesus' statement is direct and forceful, it is nevertheless wrapped in mystery.

The Greek word for "again" is *anōthen*. Born *anōthen*. It is deliberately and deliciously ambiguous. It means at least two things: to be born again and to be born from above. "Born anew" is a good translation because it preserves the ambiguity.

Nicodemus trips over the literalness of the phrase:

"How can anyone be born after having grown old? Can one enter a second time into the mother's womb and be born?" (3:4)

All through the Gospel of John, dialogues have multiple layers of meaning. There is the surface meaning, concrete and literal. And there are deeper, symbolic layers of significance. So it was with Jesus' conversation with the woman at the well in Samaria. She was talking about water from Jacob's well, and Jesus was talking about living water welling up from within (see chapter 2). Here in Jesus' dialogue with Nicodemus, we see the same sort of thing.

The idea of being born again provokes both attraction and fear in people. I recall an old *Life* magazine article with photographs of two sets of blood vessels magnified hundreds of times. One set belonged to a newborn baby. Those vessels were as smooth, slick, and clean as glass tubes. The other set belonged to an older person. Those vessels looked like old, corroded pipes—clogged and ugly, marred by too many cigarettes, ham biscuits, and fried chicken. Wouldn't it be wonderful to be able to clean those old vessels out?

Sometimes when there's a natural catastrophe, such as a flood, hurricane, or great fire, a person slips away under the cover of a presumed death and goes off to start a new life somewhere else. This life has become too painful, confused, complicated. So off the person goes to get a new identity and a fresh start. We can understand the appeal.

But that fresh start comes with fear attached. Life has accrued much to itself—credentials, possessions, position. They are part of the person. Does he or she have to give up all of that?

Likewise, spiritual conversion involves a kind of dying, dying to your false self, dying to what is diminishing your life—a life drowning in nonessentials and missing what is essential.

So for Nicodemus and for us, there is both attraction and resistance to the phrase "You must be born again."

The Mystery of New Birth

Jesus answered Nicodemus with words that present the mystery of new birth:

> "Very truly I tell you, no one can enter the kingdom of God without being born of water and Spirit. What is born of the flesh is flesh, and what is born of the Spirit is spirit." (3:5-6)

We are beginning to get the point that Jesus is pointing to a spiritual rebirth "from above." But there is mystery to the Spirit too. Jesus said to Nicodemus,

> "Do not be astonished that I said to you, 'You must be born from above.' The wind blows where it chooses, and you hear the sound of it, but you do not know where it comes from or where it goes. So it is with everyone who is born of the Spirit."

Nicodemus said to him, "How can these things be?" (3:7-9)

Nicodemus's question reveals his wonder of the meaning of Jesus' words.

The word Jesus used for Spirit is itself elusive, a triple-layered word meaning "wind," "breath," and "spirit." Jesus played on the image. The new birth is like the movement of the wind. Jesus was making an analogy, one of the deepest ways humans understand. Has anybody seen the wind? Yes, we know the wind is the movement of air molecules from high pressure to low pressure, but who can control that? Have you learned to lasso the wind? What we see is not the wind but its effects: a hat blown off, a tree swaying, a sailboat traveling, a flag waving, leaves skittering across the ground, a pinwheel spinning, a roof torn away, a tree uprooted.

You can feel the wind across your face, but you cannot say where it came from or where it is going. So it is with anyone born of the wind, breath, Spirit of God. The Spirit comes from God; you cannot manufacture the movement of the Spirit. It comes by grace; you cannot conjure it or earn it. It comes as it comes, from beyond your control.

The Various Ways of the Spirit

How variously the Spirit of God moves in our lives. For some, it moves like a cool summer breeze, sweet with the scent of flowers. For others, it moves like a swirling hurricane, shaking and rearranging everything that can be shaken so that what cannot be shaken—the essential things—remain.

For some, conversion is sudden and fierce, a 180-degree turn in an instant. A person is delivered from what is killing him or her. Often it is not pretty—not then—but it saves the person's life. It breaks like lightning from the sky. For others, conversion comes gradually, like the slow breaking of dawn.

Billy Graham said that his new birth happened dramatically. He could pinpoint the moment. For Ruth, his wife, the new birth was very different—like awakening to the light of a new day. Sometime during the night dark had turned to day. She could not pinpoint the moment. All she knew was that she now walked in the light.

William James, the renowned nineteenth-century Harvard physician, psychologist, and philosopher, wrote the first great psychology of religion, *The Varieties of Religious Experience*. In it he explored two spiritual and psychological types: the once-born and the twice-born. This typology helps us explore the various ways we are born of the Spirit.[4]

The Once-Born Person

The once-born person is the one who all life long has felt a spiritual kinship with God. God is not "holy other" but a companion within. Such persons sense God everywhere, and everything seems imbued with the goodness and presence of God. They may have experienced what Dorothee Soelle calls a "childhood mysticism." They live with a basic sense of blessing and well-being. Such people cannot remember a time when they did not consider themselves a child of God. For these people, it is as if when they breathed their first breath, they breathed God's breath too.

Conversion for the once-born is not some dramatic cataclysmic turnaround as much as the gradual growth of one who is growing in the love of God and neighbor, as a flower turns its face almost imperceptibly to the sun.

The Twice-Born Person

In contrast, twice-born persons seem to have lived always with a division of soul, or divided self. They experience to a sometimes excruciating degree the difference and distance between themselves and God. They keenly feel the struggle between good and evil inside and in the world. They have an acute, sensitive, sometimes tyrannical conscience.

Their predominant spiritual experience is not oneness with God but separateness, a sense of alienation and estrangement. Conversion for the twice-born comes as they move dramatically from estrangement to union, from alienation to oneness with God and life. Troubled souls find peace; divided selves move to wholeness and wellness of being. They have discovered what Thomas Merton called "a hidden wholeness."

The Uniqueness of Once-Born and Twice-Born

Both once-born and twice-born persons are children of God with their own spiritual uniqueness, integrity, and challenges. Whether one is once-born or twice-born may have something to do with brain biology: we are hardwired in one way or the other. Early psychological experience may also be formative for whether we live with a basic sense of well-being or a sense of dis-ease or mistrust.[5]

Different denominations and churches tend to cater more to the once-born or twice-born. The kinds of conversion they offer fit the spiritual makeup of one or the other. The kinds of spiritual experience they value and spiritual guidance they offer fit one type or the other. A once-born person may feel like a misfit in a twice-born church, and vice versa.

For some, conversion happens as it did for the apostle Paul, a twice-born person if there ever was one. He wrote, "I do not understand my own actions. For I do not do what I want, but I do the very thing I hate. . . . Wretched man that I am! Who will rescue me from this body of death?" (Romans 7:15,24). Flannery O'Connor said of Paul's conversion, "I reckon the Lord knew that the only way to make a Christian out of that one was to knock him off his horse."[6]

Dag Hammarskjöld may be a good example of the once-born. Growing up as a boy, he had a happy nature. In the 1960s he became an extraordinary world leader, secretary general of the United Nations. He was a quietly religious man with a deep mystical strain people did not know about until his spiritual journal, *Markings*, was published after his tragic death in an airplane crash while on a UN mission in Africa. He wrote these words in his journal posted on Pentecost Sunday 1961: "I don't know Who—or what—put the question. I don't know when it was put. I don't even remember answering. But at some moment I did answer *Yes* to Someone—or Something—and from that hour I was certain that existence is meaningful and that, therefore, my life in self-surrender, had a goal."[7] His conversion was as one who came to some conscious recognition of what he had known or felt at some level of his being.

The once-born and twice-born each have their spiritual challenges. The former may be tempted to spiritual complacency and a life of psychic ease, unconcerned with the needs of others. Their conversion may be a call to serve the world with the love of God. The latter may be tempted to despair over their inner psychic pain. Their conversion is to union with God and life and with a letting go of their self-despising or self-destructive patterns.

Away with Salvation Anxiety

So where does this leave us? First, I do not think the term *born again* should be used to create salvation anxiety. I've heard evangelists say things like "If you do not remember the exact moment you were saved, you may not be saved." I know Christians who worry that they've not had an apostle Paul kind of experience. Conversion requires a kind of "turning," which is what the word *repent* in the Hebrew means, a turning of the mind, which is what the word means in the Greek. But these turnings happen in so many different kinds of ways.

Jesus meant the term *born again* to be an invitation to hope: You can, we all can, be born anew. Open the windows of your life and let the Spirit blow.

Second, we should recognize that people come to God and God comes to people in a myriad of ways, each unique to the human personality. Claim the way you have come to God, or God to you, as authentically yours. Give thanks whether you are once-born or twice-born. Perhaps there is another type, the "many-born." As someone has said, it takes a lifetime of conversions to become the new creation God made us to be.

Perhaps you feel like you are some of both, once-born and twice-born. I know a woman who, as a girl, felt a deep closeness to God and would create rituals to celebrate that closeness. When she was sixteen, she joined a church that demanded a twice-born solution to her spiritual condition. The only "valid" spiritual experience, she was told, was a dramatic twice-born experience. Later in life she felt caught between the two.

Or you may have been a once-born person, and a moral crisis threw you into a period of estrangement from God and life itself. You needed a twice-born experience to feel at one with God again. A man stricken with alcoholism joins the recovery movement. "Watch me turn!" he says to his addiction.

Whether you are once-born, twice-born, or many-born, God wants you to feel God's utter belovedness however and whenever it happens. This typology cannot exhaust the mystery of the new birth. It helps us ponder it anew.

The mystery of the new birth: you cannot pin it down; you can only open yourself to its holy power.

What Happened

Did Nicodemus say yes to the new birth? The episode in John 3 does not say. But it appears that somewhere along the way he did. After Jesus was crucified, Joseph of Arimathea, a disciple, asked Pilate if he could take care of Jesus' dead body. Pilate granted his wish. Joseph took him down from the cross and carried him away. John's Gospel says next,

> Nicodemus, who had at first come to Jesus by night, also came bringing a mixture of myrrh and aloes, weighing about

a hundred pounds. They took the body of Jesus and wrapped it with the spices in linen cloths. (John 19:39-40)

Then together they laid him in the garden tomb.

Nicodemus had come to Jesus by night, and Jesus led him into the light. For all the ways the mystery of new birth happens, let us give praise and thanks.

NOTES

1. Richard Rohr, from a lecture delivered at Myers Park Baptist Church, Charlotte, NC, April, 2012.

2. Cynthia Griffin Wolf, *Emily Dickinson* (New York: Alfred A. Knopf, 1983), 87–104. These pages trace Dickinson's spiritual struggle.

3. Emily Dickenson, letter HL13.

4. William James, *The Varieties of Religious Experience* (New York: The Modern Library, 1902), 163–256.

5. The teaching of psychologist Erik Erikson has been helpful at this point.

6. Flannery O'Connor, *The Habit of Being*, ed. Sally Fitzgerald (New York: Vintage, 1979), 354–55.

7. Dag Hammarskjöld, *Markings* (New York: Alfred A. Knopf, 1966), 201.

Chapter 2

JESUS AND
the Samaritan Woman

Living Water
(John 4:1-42)

The story of the encounter between Jesus and the Samaritan woman is rich with many levels of meaning: Jesus crossing the boundaries of race, gender, and religious practice to bring God's good news; a woman married five times who becomes an apostle to the Samaritans; the universalizing of salvation from the Jews; Jesus moving the long-expected day of salvation from the future to the present. And we are just getting started. Perhaps the deepest image of the encounter comes in these words from Jesus:

> "The water that I will give will become in them a spring of water gushing up to eternal life." (4:14)

Here he describes eternal life as a spring of water welling up from deep within.

Setting the Stage

In verse 4 we are told, "[Jesus] had to go through Samaria." Samaria was the most direct route from Jerusalem to Galilee, but Jews did not like to travel through Samaria because of the animosity between Jews and Samaritans.

The people of Samaria were considered theologically incorrect, spiritually corrupt, morally unclean, and racially impure. The animosity between the Jews and Samaritans went back seven to eight hundred years. We could compare it to the animosity between Arabs and Jews in the Middle East, between Christians and Muslims since the Crusades in the eleventh, twelfth, and thirteenth centuries, or between Protestants and Catholics in Northern Ireland.

But Jesus "had to go" through Samaria. The words have theological overtones. "God so loved the world" (John 3:16), not just Jews, not just Christians, but the world. So, following the divine imperative, Jesus purposefully went through Samaria.

Beginning Conversation

Weary and thirsty, Jesus came to Jacob's well, a famous well given to the Samaritans by the patriarch Jacob himself. Today Jacob's well is identified as the hundred-foot-deep well near the base of Mount Gerizim. It was a place of great significance for the Samaritans.

A woman came to draw water at high noon—in contrast to Nicodemus, who came to Jesus under the cover of night. John is rich in symbolism, such as darkness and light.

When Jesus asked the woman for a drink of water from the well, she was startled by the request. Here was a Jewish man talking to a woman in public—a Samaritan woman, at that—and asking to drink from her "unclean" Samaritan vessels. With this request, Jesus was breaking three or four religious traditions at once.

She asked the first of a series of theological questions that had to do with the difference between Jewish theology and Samaritan theology:

"How is it that you, a Jew, ask a drink of me, a woman of Samaria?" (4:9)

John added parenthetically,

> Jews do not share things in common with Samaritans. (4:9)

Jesus answered,

> "If you knew the gift of God, and who it is that is saying to you, 'Give me a drink,' you would have asked him, and he would have given you living water." (4:10)

Jesus was speaking symbolically of spiritual things. The woman took him literally and tripped over the double meaning of "living water," just as Nicodemus tripped over the double meaning of being "born again." Living water meant running water, and it meant water that brings life. In John's Gospel, Jesus brought the light, life, and love of God.

The woman bantered back:

> "Sir, you have no bucket, and the well is deep. Where do you get that living water? Are you greater than our ancestor Jacob, who gave us the well . . . ?" (4:11-12)

Jesus answered:

> "Everyone who drinks of this water will be thirsty again, but those who drink of the water that I will give them will never be thirsty. The water that I will give will become in them a spring of water gushing up to eternal life." (4:13-14)

This scene is developing into a romance. Wells were where many Old Testament courtships began. My friend Paul Simpson Duke paints the picture: Jesus is the cowboy in the white hat and the Samaritan woman is the woman in the calico dress who bump into each other outside the general store.

But this is not a human romance; it is a sacred romance. Jesus is offering not his hand but God's hand in marriage. Jesus is the matchmaker. The water they share is living water streaming from God's heart through Jesus' heart into her heart. And it wells up from deep within because God's streaming river of love and life flows not just in the heavens but deep within each of us.

The woman answered:

> "Sir, give me this water, so that I may never be thirsty."(4:15)

This is the water we all want. We are all thirsty for God, for a deeper, fuller, truer life.

The Deepening Conversation

Jesus then abruptly changed the subject:

> "Go, call your husband, and come back." The woman answered him, "I have no husband." Jesus said to her, "You are right in saying 'I have no husband'; for you have had five husbands, and the one you have now is not your husband." (4:16-18)

Jesus then applauded her honesty:

> "What you have said is true!" (4:18)

Often at this point, the discussion of the woman turns moralistic with the suggestion that the woman was highly immoral and that her sins were sexual in nature. This is an almost pornographic reduction of the woman into a sexual object.

In truth, the fact that she had had five husbands need not suggest immorality. It may have reflected her victimization as a woman in a patriarchal culture.[1] Had she been discarded by five husbands? By the law of levirate marriage, had she been passed from family member to family member to bear children? Had she failed to bear children, and thus been passed over?

Jesus makes no moral judgment. He does not say to her, "Go, and sin no more." He does not shame her. He meets her person to person, preserving her dignity.

The Woman's Theological Conversation

The woman is set free to continue her theological conversation with Jesus:

> "Sir, I see that you are a prophet." (4:19)

How else could he know her life? With Mount Gerizim towering over them, she added:

> "Our ancestors worshiped on this mountain, but you [Jews] say that the place where people must worship is in Jerusalem." (4:20)

This line of questioning was not meant—as too many sermons suggest—as an attempt to divert the conversation away from her sinful past. It was the continuance of a theological conversation made possible by Jesus' non-shaming, dignity-giving presence.

Here was the heart of the conflict between Samaritans and Jews: where and how to worship. The Samaritans had built a holy shrine on Mount Gerizim that was destroyed by Jewish troops in 128 BCE. Here was not an academic question. It carried centuries of religious rivalry and hostility.

Jesus answered with his longest theological statement:

> "Woman, believe me, the hour is coming when you will worship the Father neither on this mountain nor in Jerusalem. You worship what you do not know; we worship what we know, for salvation is from the Jews. But the hour is coming, and is now here, when the true worshipers will worship the Father in spirit and truth, for the Father seeks such as these to worship him. God is spirit, and those who worship him must worship in spirit and truth." (4:21-24)

Thinking of the age to come when the Messiah will come, the woman said,

"I know that the Messiah is coming. . . . When he comes, he will proclaim all things to us." (4:25)

Jesus, invoking the divine name Yahweh, or I AM WHAT I AM, answered,

"I am he, the one who is speaking to you." (4:26).

Jesus was bringing God's "eternal now" to the woman. The age to come is here and now. True worship will not be confined to a holy place, Jerusalem or Gerizim, because the true God cannot be contained in a holy place. Worship happens anywhere God is worshipped in spirit and truth.

Jesus made clear that "salvation is from the Jews" (4:22). Seeing Jesus or the salvation he brings apart from his Jewishness is a terrible distortion. But salvation is not limited to the Jews. It was coming to the Samaritans and to the whole world. No longer do we draw a line between chosen people and rejected people. All are chosen in love. We have moved from a faith too "local," too confining, to a gospel that is more universal.

The woman's theological questioning led Jesus to offer sublime theological answers.

The Disciples' Response

Just as Jesus revealed his messianic identity to the woman, the disciples barged in like the Keystone Kops. They had been out looking for food, and when they returned they saw Jesus talking with a woman. A woman! They were shocked: Jesus talking in public with a woman, and a Samaritan woman at that! But, as the text reveals, no one challenged Jesus, saying, "Why are you speaking with her?" (verse 27). They'd probably had this conversation before. The disciples then, as many disciples now, could not accept the spiritual equality of women. Women's inferiority is encased in tradition, liturgy, and biblical interpretation—from the Vatican to the Southern Baptist Convention. The church is so often captive to its culture.

The Woman as Apostle

The encounter now took a startling turn. The woman left her water jar (symbolically she didn't need the bucket; she now had living water) and returned to her village an apostle of Christ to the Samaritans. She exclaimed:

> "Come and see . . . ! "He cannot be the Messiah, can he?" (4:29)

Here is the heart of our evangelical mission: to point people to Christ and say, "Come and see." "Come and see," as Philip, earlier in John said, introducing Jesus to Nathanael (John 1:46).

Sure enough, the Samaritans to whom the woman spoke made their way to Jesus. And the text says,

> Many Samaritans from that city believed in him because of the woman's testimony" (4:39).

They even asked Jesus to come and stay with them in their city. Jesus did, and many more believed.

> They said to the woman: "It is no longer because of what you said that we believe, for we have heard for ourselves, and we know that this is truly the Savior of the world." (4:42)

Savior of the world! This is where the story had been headed from the beginning.

Here we have the astonishing story of Jesus crossing racial, national, gender, and religious lines to offer the gift of eternal life to a Samaritan woman, then making her his apostle to the Samaritans! Jesus' saviorhood was reaching throughout the world.

Living Water

In Willa Cather's classic *Death Comes for the Archbishop*, she tells the tale, based on the history of the American Southwest, of Father Latour, a French priest who was sent by the Roman Catholic Church to be archbishop over the area of Santa Fe and New Mexico.

In one episode an Indian guide, Jacinto, was guiding Father Latour through a snowstorm in the New Mexico wilderness. Father Latour began to fear for his life. Jacinto led them up a cliff to a small opening in a rock. They crawled through the mouth in the rock and found themselves in a cave. When they built a fire, Father Latour saw that they were in a great cavernous underground area that looked in the flickering light like a Gothic cathedral. They had entered an ancient Indian holy place.

Father Latour began to hear a dizzying noise in his head. At first he thought he was experiencing vertigo or some roaring in his inner ear. Here is Cather's description:

> But as he grew warm and relaxed, he perceived an extraordinary vibration in this cavern; it hummed like a hive of bees, like a heavy roll of distant drums. After a time he asked Jacinto whether he, too, noticed this. The slim Indian boy smiled. . . . He took up a . . . torch, and beckoned the Padre to follow him along a tunnel. . . . There Jacinto knelt down over a fissure in the stone floor, like a crack in china, which was plastered up with clay. Digging some of this out with his hunting knife, he put his ear on the opening, listened for a few seconds, and motioned the Bishop to do likewise.
>
> Father Latour lay with his ear to this crack for a long while, despite the cold that arose from it. He told himself he was listening to one of the oldest voices of the earth. What he heard was the sound of a great underground river, flowing through a resounding cavern. The water was far, far below, perhaps as deep as the foot of the mountain, a flood

moving in utter blackness under the ribs of the antediluvian rock. It was not a rushing noise, but the sound of a great flood moving with majesty and power.[2]

"I give you living water welling up to eternal life," Jesus says, beckoning us, placing his own ear to the surface of our souls, then inviting us to do the same and hear the great river of life flowing deep inside.

If you place your ear there, you will hear that great river. You will hear a voice as ancient as the earth, whispering, *You are my beloved. Live in my love. You are my apostle. Spread that love. It is saving the world.*

Epilogue

New Testament scholar Sandra Schneiders identifies a historical layer to the text that gives us something important to ponder.[3] The story of the Samaritan woman, she writes, was used to direct the church's early mission to the Samaritans. Jesus was calling them from the worship of false gods to the worship of the one true God. The Hebrew prophets often called Israel away from false gods they had taken as lovers.

When the Samaritans returned from Assyrian captivity, they carried with them the false gods of the five countries around Assyria's border. The list in 2 Kings 17:29-31 names them:

1. The people of Babylon made Succoth-benoth.

2. The people of Cuth made Nergal.

3. The people of Hamath made Ashima.

4. The Avvites made Nibhaz and Tartak.

5. And the Sepharvites burned their children in the fire to Adrammelech and Anammelech.

The woman's five husbands stood symbolically for the false gods of these five nations who had become husbands to Samaria rather than Yahweh. Some followed these gods in addition to Yahweh. The prophet was calling them to the exclusive worship of Yahweh.

What are the gods we worship in America today? Roger Williams, the founder of the Baptist movement in North America, in his colorful seventeenth-century language, named the false gods of his day: "The truth is, the great Gods of this world are God-belly, God-peace, God-wealth, God-honour, God-pleasure, etc."[4]

How would we describe them today?

God-power

God-land

God-nation

God-race

God-money

I've heard that the four core addictions are these:

1. Control
2. Sensation
3. Suffering
4. Security

These promise pleasure but bring pain.

Jesus through this story was calling the Samaritans away from the worship of the false gods that they served in addition to Yahweh. So it is with us: we want our false gods along with the true one. But this will not work. We become divided selves. If we build our lives around one or more of these false gods, we will forfeit the eternal life offered us in Christ, a life characterized by wholeness, peace, and the love of God and neighbor.

Jesus the matchmaker is calling us to the wholehearted, undivided worship of God, truly "in spirit and in truth."

NOTES

1. Feminist biblical scholars are giving us new eyes to see old texts. In this chapter, I am indebted to the work of two scholars, especially Sandra Schneiders, *Written That You May Believe: Encountering Jesus in the Fourth Gospel* (New York: Herder and Herder, 2001), 126–48; Gail O'Day, *John*, The Interpreter's Bible, vol. 14 (Nashville: Abingdon, 1995), 5612–73.

2. Willa Cather, *Death Comes for the Archbishop* (New York: Alfred A. Knopf, 1926), 131–32.

3. Schneiders, *Written That You May Believe*, 137–41.

4. Mary Lee Settle, *I, Roger Williams* (New York: Norton, 2001), 24.

Chapter 3

JESUS AND
the Man by the Pool

"Wilt Thou Be Made Whole?"
(John 5:1-9)

A miracle of healing happened near the Sheep Gate in Jerusalem by the pool of Beth-zatha (other translations say Bethesda or Bethsaida). Many invalids were lying by the pool, blind, lame, sick, and paralyzed, wishing, wanting, waiting to be healed. They believed that when the waters were stirred, it was an angel who stirred the waters, and if a person got into the pool at that moment, he or she would be healed.

One man by the pool had been paralyzed for thirty-eight years. No one knows how many times he had prayed to be healed and almost given up. But here he was trying again. And Jesus asked him the penetrating question: "Wilt thou be made whole?" (5:6, KJV). Or, as the New Revised Standard Version translates it: "Do you want to be made well?"

Jesus the Healer

We may carry some modern skepticism with us about Jesus the healer. Thomas Jefferson did. He believed Jesus was a great moral teacher but not a supernatural healer, so when he edited the Gospels to make his own "Life of Jesus," he took out the miracles. Other scholars have done the same since. But if you cut all of the miracles out of the Gospels with scissors, what remains looks like what is left of a piece of paper once you have cut out paper dolls. For example, in the first chapter of Mark alone, we have one exorcism, two healings, and a report of many other miracles—almost half of the verses.

Yes, Jesus was a great moral teacher, but he was (and is) more. He was a prophet of justice and a friend of sinners. He was the Lamb of God who takes away the sin of the world. He was Son of God and Son of Man, but he was a healer too. Not just the Good Shepherd but also the Great Physician.

New Testament scholar Obery Hendricks writes, "Throughout his ministry, Jesus treated the people and their needs as holy by healing their bodies, their souls, their psyches."[1] Your needs are holy to God.

Jesus not only healed every kind of illness but also healed anybody who came to be healed: Jew, Gentile, sinner, righteous, rich, poor, men, women, and children. (And he never made a moral demand of a person before healing them.) He never said, "If you shape up, I'll heal you." The only requirement was a recognition of need and enough faith to crack open the door to God's grace. Sometimes God cracked open the door.

Jesus' healings were more than physical: he healed minds, emotions, and spirits too. Why did he heal? Over and over again, the answer was his compassion. Out of God's tender mercies he healed people—and in the power of God's Spirit manifested as the kingdom drew near.

In Matthew's Gospel alone, the Evangelist records fifteen individual healings:

> a leper,
>
> a centurion's paralyzed servant,
>
> Peter's mother-in-law with a fever (yes, mothers-in-law too!),
>
> a paralyzed man,

the daughter of Jairus,

the woman with the flow of blood,

two blind men,

a demoniac unable to speak,

the Canaanite woman's daughter possessed of a demon,

a man with a withered hand,

a man blind and mute,

a man's epileptic son, and

two more blind men

Then there are, by my count, twelve descriptions of groups being healed:

the lame,

the deaf,

people with seizures,

the maimed,

the mute,

lepers,

the paralyzed,

those with evil spirits,

those harassed and helpless,

those trapped in sin,

those walking in the shadow of death; and

he fed the hungry multitude (this was a miracle too, a social miracle—God wants people fed).

How many ways are there to be a leper, paralyzed, blind, mute, deaf, maimed, heartsick, soul-sick, sin-sick? Jesus healed all maladies. Out of his boundless compassion, he healed them. Even the great Jewish historian of that day, Josephus, himself not a follower of Jesus, called Jesus "a doer of startling deeds."[2] Yes, Jesus was a healer, and he is a healer still.

The kingdom of God that Jesus preached means many things: justice, joy, peace, radical inclusion, forgiveness, reconciliation, home. But it also means healing. God's will is for all of God's children to be whole. The prophet Jeremiah cried out, "Is there no balm in Gilead? Is there no physician there?" (Jeremiah 8:22). Yes, there is. And his name is Jesus.

The Meeting

Back to our text and the paralyzed man by the pool. When Jesus saw him, he knew the man had been there a long time. Did he see how weak the man was? The hopelessness in his eyes? Jesus notices us and knows us. He knows how long we've struggled. He knows us better than we know ourselves. And he comes to our aid.

Jesus then asked the man the question he knew the man needed most to answer: "Do you want to be healed? Wilt thou be made whole?" It was a penetrating, unavoidable question. Do you really want healing? Are you willing to do whatever it takes? Will you trust? Go for broke?

The man may have thought, *What do you mean, do I want to be healed? I'm here by the pool, aren't I?* But sometimes we place ourselves around the edges of God's power, on the back row, close but not close enough.

The man answered out of his passivity and helplessness. After thirty-eight years, who could blame him?

> "Sir, I have no one to put me into the pool when the water
> is stirred up; and while I am making my way, someone else
> steps down ahead of me."(5:7)

Where were those to help him into the pool? Where is the church? That's what the church should be about: helping each other get into the pool.

Sometimes we've reached that point. Passive. Helpless. Ready to give up. *Don't give up!*

Jesus spoke:

"Stand up, take your mat and walk!" At once the man was made well, and he took up his mat and began to walk. (5:8-9)

He didn't even need the water. All he needed was Jesus.

Are We That Man?

I am that man beginning to walk. Let me explain. For years I have experienced this text through the playwright Thornton Wilder and the apostle Paul.

In Thornton Wilder's play based on this story, *The Angel That Troubled the Waters*, Wilder paints us this picture. A disabled physician is waiting by the pool with all the others. An angel comes and stirs the waters. As the physician moves toward the water, the angel says, "Draw back, physician, this moment is not for you. . . . Without your wound where would your power be? It is your very remorse that makes your low voice tremble in the hearts of men. The very angels themselves cannot persuade the wretched and blundering children on earth as one human being broken on the wheels of the living. In Love's Service only the wounded soldiers can serve."[3] That has been my story for many years, the physician who could not be healed, not fully so, but who ministered as God's "wounded healer."

Henri Nouwen came up with this image of the wounded healer based on an old Jewish story. Someone asked, "Where is the Messiah?" The answer came. "He is in the middle of the village, wrapping and unwrapping his bandages one at a time so that he can also minister to others around him."[4] This is a profound image of the church. We are the broken, wounded body of Christ. Through our brokenness and woundedness, we minister to others. We are like cracked earthen vessels letting God's grace flow from us, through us, to others.

The apostle Paul was a wounded healer. He had what he called a "thorn in the flesh." We don't know what it was, but it was an agonizing and humiliating affliction. He prayed over and over for the thorn to be removed, but it was not. What he received instead was this answer:

"My grace is sufficient for you, for my power is made perfect in weakness." (2 Corinthians 12:9, RSV)

This is the beautiful mystery of the gospel: strength made perfect in weakness. Paul was given the grace to bear his affliction. "When thro' fi'ry trials thy pathway shall lie, My grace, all-sufficient, shall be thy supply."[5] And more, his weakness would be a vessel for God's strength. How did Paul put it?

But we have this treasure in earthen vessels, to show that the transcendent power belongs to God and not to us. (2 Corinthians 4:7, RSV)

Wounded healers: that's who we are, God using our brokenness to heal others. For many years my "thorn," my affliction, has been in part depression, which sometimes has felt like a "sickness unto death." The psalmist described depression as "the destruction that wastes at noonday" (Psalm 91:6). In the middle of a bright sunny day, it can feel darker than a hundred midnights. Feeling that I needed more help, a few years ago I went off for a month into the care of physicians and counselors. Ministers need help sometimes too. You could say I went to the pool of Bethesda.

During that month of care, I went into a chapel one day by myself. I opened the Bible, and there it was: John 5 and the story of the man by the pool. And this is what I heard: not an angel saying, "Draw back, physician, healing is not for you," but God saying, "Draw back no more. Healing is for you too, Steve. Do you hear me? Healing is for you."

God had more healing for me than I thought. I am that man walking the road to wholeness. Not all at once, but step by step I am on the road to wholeness. Sometimes healings take some time. One of my favorite healing stories is the blind man who needed a two-stage healing. (I deal with this story in chapter 8.) Jesus placed his spittle on the man's eyes, then asked what he could see. The man said he could see a little, but men looked like trees walking! So Jesus did it again. He anointed the man's eyes a second time, and this time the man could see clearly. Sometimes healing is a journey and wholeness a process.

Like the old man said, "I'm not what I want to be. I'm not what I'm going to be, but thank God, I'm not what I used to be!" You see, I had almost given up on healing. I thought I had received all I was going to get. But then came the word, "Draw back no more. Healing is for you too!"

Do you want to be healed? Wilt thou be made whole? God is at work every day to heal us body, mind, and spirit and make us whole. God has goodness in store for us. What does the psalmist say? "Goodness and mercy shall follow me all the days of my life" (Psalm 23:6).

A month after receiving this word, I was in Jerusalem at the very place the miracle in our text happened: by the Sheep Gate at the pool. And I heard the word all over again. "Healing is for you too."

And here we are, all of us, by the Sheep Gate at the pool of Bethesda. Jesus comes by and notices us. He knows how long we've suffered. He asks the unavoidable question, "Wilt thou be made whole?" And before we can finish all our excuses, he says, "Rise, take up your pallet and walk!"

Afterword

"Sir, I have no one to put me into the pool," the paralyzed man said. These words speak a question to the church. Are you involved with the healing ministry of Jesus? Are you helping bring people to Jesus' healing waters?

When Jesus sent the disciples out on mission, he sent them not just to preach the good news of the kingdom but also to heal (Matthew 10:7-8). A case could be made that the church has answered the call to preach more faithfully than we have answered the call to heal. As we offer Jesus to the world, we are called to carry the healing ministry of Jesus to the world.

The Iona Community off the coast of Scotland has a weekly healing ministry that has deeply moved me. Every Tuesday evening, as part of their evening worship service, they invite people to come to the front of the sanctuary to receive the laying on of hands. As these persons kneel in a circle, the congregation surrounds them, lays on hands, and prays this prayer aloud for each one:

Spirit of the Living God,
Present with us now,
Enter your body, mind and spirit,
And heal you of all that harms you,
In Jesus' name. Amen.[6]

Might we, in our own ways, pray such a prayer and offer the healing ministry of Jesus to one another and to the world?

NOTES

1. Obery M. Hendricks Jr., *The Politics of Jesus* (New York: Doubleday, 2006), 108.

2. Josephus, Jewish Antiquities, 18:63-4.

3. Thornton Wilder, *The Angel That Troubled the Waters* (New York: Coward McCann, 1928), 145.

4. Henri Nouwen, *The Wounded Healer: Ministry in Contemporary Society* (New York: Doubleday, 1972), 83–84.

5. John Rippon, "How Firm a Foundation."

6. *Iona Abbey Worship Book* (Glasgow: Wild Goose, 2001), 91.

Chapter 4

JESUS AND
the Canaanite Woman

When Jesus Changed His Mind
(Matthew 15:21-28)

The extraordinary encounter between Jesus and a Canaanite woman has more surprise in it than most any story in the Gospels I can think of. Matthew 15:21-28 tells of a foreign woman's tenacious faith, which changed Jesus' mind, not only about healing her daughter but also about the direction of his mission in the world.

Hers was a faith passionate and persistent, unafraid to joust with God, a faith that would not settle for life's noes but trusted in a deeper yes. And Jesus? It is said of a true servant-leader that he or she has the capacity to be influenced as well as to influence. Jesus was turned in a new direction by this woman's remarkable and surprising faith.

The Weary Jesus

The encounter began as Jesus was trying to escape for a brief rest. He was tired and beleaguered by the demands of his ministry and by the opposition he was facing from his own people, the house of Israel. Just a few chapters before, we read these foreboding words from Jesus: "Prophets are not without

honor except in their own country and in their own house"
(13:57). Then Matthew concluded, "And he did not do many
deeds of power there, because of their unbelief" (verse 58).

In the scene preceding this chapter's story, Jesus became
involved in a confrontation over the application of the law
and said, "So for the sake of your tradition, you make void
the word of God" (15:6). Such is the danger of religious
tradition.

No wonder Jesus needed rest! So he headed for the district
of Tyre and Sidon, Gentile territory. Maybe there he would
find peace and quiet.

The Encounter

As Jesus entered that territory, a Canaanite woman came to
him and started shouting,

> "Have mercy on me, Lord, Son of David; my daughter is
> tormented by a demon." (15:22)

She was a Canaanite, a Gentile, an Arab, a pagan, unclean. She
was beyond the pale. But her daughter was in torment, and her
love for her sick daughter was its own kind of faith. T. S. Eliot
wrote of "the purification of the motive / In the ground of our
beseeching."[1] This woman was at the ground of her beseeching. She would go anywhere, do anything to help her daughter.

She must have heard about the compassionate prophet
who healed people, so she came before him and started
shouting her plea. She wanted his attention: "Have mercy
on me, Lord, Son of David. My daughter needs help."

It is interesting that she, a Canaanite, called Jesus by a
Jewish messianic title, but when your daughter is desperate, you are desperate. You'll borrow money and go to
Johns Hopkins, or hop a plane to Mexico for some experi-
mental treatment, or go to a faith healer you had formerly
scorned. I visited a woman years ago who was about to

have a dangerous ten-hour surgery. I asked if I could pray with her, for her. "Yes," she answered, "I'd take voodoo at this moment." Then she added with a smile, "You can get real ecumenical at a time like this." This Canaanite woman would even approach a Jewish stranger and call him "Lord, Son of David."

Silence Can Be Deafening

What was Jesus' response to the woman's plea? The text is blunt:

But he did not answer her at all. (15:23)

(Who has not experienced the silence of Heaven?) You cry out for help, pray for guidance, plead for a miracle, but receive only silence. You hear: God answers all our prayers, sometimes yes, sometimes no, sometimes not yet. That is scarce comfort.

Why was Jesus silent? Was he pondering what to do, how to answer? Whatever the reason, his silence must have felt like a no. God's silence can be deafening.

The disciples rushed in to end the silence and to rescue Jesus from this unclean woman and her need:

"Send her away, for she keeps shouting after us." (15:23)

"We came here to *rest*, Jesus. Take a rest. Be done with this nuisance of a woman!" Sometimes our compassion reaches its limit. We are afraid to minister to a person because of her or his bottomless neediness. The disciples were trying to protect Jesus, and perhaps they were also trying to protect themselves. Did the fact that the woman was a pagan Gentile, unclean Arab play into their callous response?

So now the woman had heard a second no—first Jesus' silence, now the cruel dismissal of the disciples: "Send her away."

Jesus then speaks, and what he speaks is another no:

"I was sent only to the lost sheep of the house of Israel."
(15:24)

His words were perfectly consistent with the purpose of his
mission, which he had stated before. When he sent his disciples
out on missions, he charged them, "Go nowhere among the
Gentiles, and enter no town of the Samaritans, but go rather to
the lost sheep of the house of Israel" (Matthew 10:5-6). Jesus
had set the trajectory of his mission as he understood it: to go
after the lost sheep of the house of Israel, the poor, the sinners,
those lost on their way.

A third no. Could the woman have heard his words in any
other way?

But she persisted. Trusting in a merciful and true God, she
asked again. Kneeling before Jesus, she said,

"Lord, help me." (15:25)

The desert fathers and mothers instructed us about how
to pray. When all the prayers we pray have run out, they
taught, say, "Lord, help!" That will be enough.

Then Jesus answered in a way that feels so wrong we want
to dismiss the whole story. He quoted a proverb:

"It is not fair to take the children's food and throw it to the
dogs." (15:26)

Perhaps the proverb had its place: Feed the children first, then
the pets. But it feels cruel at this moment with the Canaanite
woman asking for help. Was Jesus calling her a dog?

How we wish we could have been there to hear the inflec-
tion in his voice, to see his facial expressions. In these old
texts, we get the words but not always the music. How could
she not have heard it as but a thundering no? The *fourth* no
in succession!

What did the woman do? She answered with a feisty retort, using the proverb but turning it on its head:

"Yes, Lord, yet even the dogs eat the crumbs that fall from their masters' table." (15:27)

This clever, brave, tenacious woman would not give up. She stood up to Jesus' no and answered both humbly and audaciously, "Yet even the dogs eat the crumbs that fall." In other words, "Israel may have the whole feast, but for my daughter's sake I'll take the crumbs!"

Where have you heard life's noes? From early childhood, so that you hear the reverberation of rejection everywhere? When the most important person in your life walked out of your life? When your dreams were ridiculed?

Have you heard the church's no and taken it to be God's no? Sometimes the church acts like the disciples in the story: as gatekeepers of the grace of God—and stingy gatekeepers, at that. Grace is never stingy, always extravagant, which is a lesson the church sometimes need to learn. As Annie Dillard wrote: "You catch grace as a man fills his cup under a waterfall."[2] Somehow this woman had the faith to trust in a deeper yes than all the noes she had experienced. This woman's faith is breathtaking. She trusted in a deeper yes that lay beneath, beyond all the noes. As Martin Luther said, she held on to the "deep and secret 'yea' beneath and above the 'nay.'"[3]

Jesus Turning

Jesus' response to this woman's words is a surprise turn in the story:

"Woman, great is your faith! Let it be done for you as you wish." And her daughter was healed instantly. (15:28)

This woman's tenacious, passionate, feisty faith changed Jesus' mind. He had the capacity to be influenced, just as we have the ability to influence. The God of the Bible is not the "unmoved mover" of Greek philosophy but a God capable of being moved. This woman's faith startled Jesus into a new direction. Not only did her faith change his mind about her daughter; it also changed the direction of his mission: beyond the lost sheep of the house of Israel to lost sheep everywhere. The house of Israel was expanding its walls.

Jesus had come to this chance meeting beleaguered by the demands of his work and by the opposition he was increasingly experiencing. But now he met the surprising faith of this Canaanite woman and his mission changed its course.

Jesus would go to Samaria and meet a Samaritan woman (see chapter 2); he would heal a Gadarene demoniac; he would heal a Samaritan leper who, alone among the ten lepers healed, would come back to praise God and thank Jesus. He would heal a Roman centurion's son/servant and say, "In no one in Israel have I found such faith" (Matthew 8:10). And in the miracle of resurrection life, he would send his disciples not only to the lost sheep of the house of Israel but into "all nations" (Matthew 28:19).

This story poses a question to the church: is our mission too limited? Have we decided on the "lost sheep" we are willing to help and closed our hearts to others? I once heard Barbara Brown Taylor say in a sermon that the signs on church lawns saying "All Are Welcome" frequently have the truth-in-advertising value of those signs in supermarkets that say "Vine Ripe Tomatoes." Could God be surprising you with a new turn in your ministry?

The Woman's Faith

Let's reflect on this woman's faith. She endured four noes until she received God's yes. She trusted in the goodness of a God she barely knew. Paul Tillich spoke of a "God beyond God," the God beyond the gods of our religions and cultures. This woman trusted in this "God beyond God," in the faithfulness at the heart of things.

Her story reminds me of Jacob's wrestling with the angel at the River Jabbok. They wrestled all night long, a wrestling as for one's own life. Finally, the angel said, "Let me go." Jacob replied, "I will not let you go, unless you bless me" (Genesis 32:26). Then the angel gave Jacob a new name, Israel, "for you have striven with God and humans, and have prevailed" (verse 28). Then the angel blessed him. Jacob named the place Peniel, "For I have seen God face to face, and yet my life is preserved" (verse 30).

Has the Canaanite woman's life of faith been like yours? Wrestling with God, with Jesus, with the Bible until you are blessed? Searching for the yes of God amid all the noes because down deep you believe there is a yes somewhere?

This woman wrestled with Jesus and saw the face of God. Like Jacob, she, too, would not leave without being blessed. And she became in the encounter a daughter of Israel, that old wrestler with God. Might we say she became a new Israel founded on sheer faith, on a trust that beyond every no, life can bring a deeper yes, the eternal yes of God revealed in the face of Jesus?

NOTES

1. T. S. Eliot, *Four Quartets* (New York: A Harvest Book, 1943), 57.

2. Annie Dillard, *Pilgrim at Tinker Creek* (NY: Harper and Row, 1974), 81

3. Martin Luther, quoted in Karl Barth, *Church Dogmatics*, I.1 (Edinburgh: T&T Clark, 1936), 203.

Chapter 5

JESUS AND the Woman Taken in Adultery

"Where Are Your Accusers?" (John 8:1-11)

In John 8:1-11 we find an encounter that is part of the indelible memory of the church: Jesus and the woman taken in adultery. She is first of all a woman "taken" (8:3, KJV).

This text, however, is not to be found in the Revised Common Lectionary adopted by many denominations, and therefore it is rarely preached. It is a scene as familiar as "Jesus and the children" or "Jesus cleansing the temple," but it is rarely read in worship anymore.

Why was it omitted? Squeamishness over the topic, perhaps, a "scarlet letter" story? Was it because scholars now know that the text was not included in the earliest manuscripts of John's Gospel? Today it is placed in brackets or footnotes in some Bibles. It seems to have been an orphan text floating around looking for a home, important to the early church, but nobody knew where to place it. In some ancient manuscripts, it shows up in other places in John (after John 7:36) and in Luke's Gospel (after Luke 21:38). The text is so representative of Jesus' character and so important to the memory of the church that church leaders did not want it to disappear.

I was given a new door to this text in Mary Gordon's book *Reading Jesus: A Writer's Encounter with the Gospels.*[1] Gordon is a noted novelist, raised Roman Catholic, who was riding in a New York City taxicab one day and heard on the radio a mean-spirited sermon on Jesus' parable of the sheep and the goats. The incident propelled her to get out of the taxi and read straight through the Gospels for herself. And from that reading came her book. Her chapter on this story gave me new eyes to see it and new ears to hear it and propelled me to ponder it again.

Here is the story, as vivid and memorable as Jesus' parables of the prodigal son and the good Samaritan.

The Accusers

Jesus was in Jerusalem teaching near the temple to an interested crowd when a woman was dragged into his presence and forced to "stand before all of them" (8:3).

She had been "taken" (KJV) in adultery. "Caught" (NRSV) is the normal translation, but the action was more violent than just "caught." *Katalambanō*: she was taken, as by force, maybe to that bed, but surely from that bed, and dragged into public and made to stand in the middle of the crowd in front of Jesus. Did the men let her dress? Did they watch her? She was placed in front of the people like an object, and the language here reveals that a kind of violence was done to her.

"Where was the guy?" we might ask. "Where was the fornicating man?" How arbitrarily, subjectively, society chooses its chief sinners and those who are to be punished.

The scribes and Pharisees said to Jesus:

> "Teacher, this woman was caught in the very act of committing adultery. Now in the law Moses commanded us to stone such women. Now what do you say?" (8:4-5)

They said those words to "test" Jesus, so "that they might have some charge to bring against him."

She is being used. Gordon comments that she is "a plaything, a pawn."[2] She is without power, easy to scorn, easy prey for those who want to use her as a theological pawn, a political pawn, as people are also used today.

And at the cost of a life! On October 26, 2018, Matthew Sheperd's ashes were interred at the National Cathedral in Washington, DC, twenty years after he was brutally beaten, his five-foot-two-inch hundred-and-five-pound body tied to a fence post and left to die—just because he was gay. He was 21 years old. Thousands of black men were lynched in the South, the lynchings accompanied by Christian hymns, like "The Old Rugged Cross" and Christian symbols. Six million Jews were killed during the Holocaust and are still killed today, as in the murder of eleven Jews as they worshiped in Pittsburgh, all in the name of religion, race, nation, and morality.

They made her "stand before all of them." In Gordon's words, "Unflanked. Unprotected. Alone."[3] Except that she was placed before Jesus, so she was not alone. She would never be alone.

The accusers said,

> "Now in the law Moses commanded us to stone such women." (8:5)

Gordon comments, "Such. Such a one. . . . Her name is 'such.' We hear the demand that as a 'such' violence be perpetrated upon her, as a deterrent to her 'suches,' others of her kind. The loudness, the force of the accusation is followed by the invocation of a law."[4] We see it happen all the time: people reduced to a "such." "He is such a. . . ." "She is such a. . . ." A nationally known radio personality called Georgetown University law student Sandra Fluke a "slut" and a "prostitute" after she had testified to Congress about access to birth control.[5] People of the right and the left use slurs to describe their political opponents. We could make a long list of epithets—racial, sexual, political, class-based, and religious—that people use to demean and dehumanize, to reduce people to their "suchness." American culture is riven by hate-filled speech. Whole groups of people can be scapegoated, dragged into the public arena to bring in votes and money. Hate is a money maker in politics and religion.

The Response of Jesus

What did Jesus do? The trap had been set. Would he be seen as easy on sin, a disregarder of the Mosaic law, undependable as a moral teacher, or would he give the woman back into the hands of the righteous keepers of the law?

Jesus did not immediately answer the woman's accusers. As she stood there, he knelt and wrote something in the sand. What did he write? Note first that he *knelt* there beside the woman. The accusers stood around her, but Jesus knelt beside her. Many suggestions have been made about what he wrote. Imagining what he might have written is a wonderful spiritual exercise. What do you imagine he wrote? What would you have wanted him to write?

Some say he was doodling there in the sand, buying some time while he figured out what to say, or extending the silence to make the accusers squirm a little longer. Maybe he scribbled a message for the woman—something just between the two of them. Maybe he wrote the most oft-repeated word of God to us in Scripture: "Be not afraid." I smile at the thought: *Be not afraid. You are not alone.*

Then Jesus stood up and said the words that are the vivid collective memory of the church:

> "Let anyone among you who is without sin be the first to throw a stone at her." (8:7)

Jesus was acting out his words from the Sermon on the Mount: "Do not judge, so that you may not be judged" (Matthew 7:1).

An early version of this story circulated in the first centuries. It pictured Jesus draping his body over the woman's to protect her from the stones. This image does not belong to the original story, but how much like Jesus it would be, to protect those judged and hated by society even with his own body. The cross itself is an image of Jesus draping his body over all humanity and their sins, giving us a new chance.

Now it was the crowd's turn to be silent. And as they heard Jesus' words, the text says,

"They went away, one by one, beginning with the elders." (8:9)

"At this moment," Gordon writes, "an entire ethical system is born."[6] It undercuts the prevailing system where sexual sin is elevated above all others. Dorothy Sayers, the famous British mystery novelist and Christian writer, wrote an essay on the seven deadly sins titled "The Other Six Deadly Sins." The title came from the time she mentioned the seven deadly sins in a lecture at Oxford and a young man came and said, "I did not know there were seven deadly sins. Please tell me the names of the other six."[7]

So Jesus leveled the playing field of sins. He also implied that we can never judge another from a position of moral superiority. As 1 John says, "If we say that we have no sin, we deceive ourselves, and the truth is not in us" (1:8). The church too often divides the world into the righteous and the wicked, the good and the despicable, and pronounces its judgment, its condemnation. We exalt ourselves, making ourselves "separate and superior."[8] The famous Duke novelist Reynolds Price was a devoted follower of Jesus, but he would not join a church because of its proclivity to judge, thereby betraying the spirit of Jesus. He wrote these stirring, challenging words:

Orthodox Christianity, the church in most of its past and present forms, has defaced and even reversed whole broad aspects of Jesus' teaching; but in no case has the church turned more culpably from his aim and his practice than in its hateful rejection of what it sees as outcasts: the whores and cheats, the traitors and killers, the baffled and stunned, the social outlaw, the maimed and hideous and contagious. If it is possible to discern, in the gospel documents of Mark and John, a conscious goal that sent the man Jesus—himself an urgent function of the Maker of all—to his agonized death, can we detect a surer aim than his first and last announced intent to sweep the lost with him into God's coming reign?[9]

Jesus and the Woman

But the encounter was not yet at an end. Jesus knelt down a second time and wrote something. What was it this time? Then he stood up and asked the woman,

> "Woman, where are they? Has no one condemned you?" She said, "No one, sir." And Jesus said, "Neither do I condemn you. Go your way, and from now on do not sin again." (8:10-11)

Maybe what Jesus wrote this time was, first, "Do not be afraid." Then "Do not be ashamed." Or "No condemnation!" Not from others, not from him, for Jesus is God.

He closed their conversation with the words "Go your way, and from now on do not sin again." Does this feel like he has set the bar impossibly high? Who could pull this off?

Or was he speaking of this particular sin? Was he saying, "Remember and learn. Do not fall back into that again"?

In a new class in a federal prison, an English teacher taught literary classics to the inmates. Some questioned what good classical literature would be to inmates. Teach something more practical, please! But the teacher argued, "What great fiction does is to help us imagine a 'before' and an 'after,' the possibility of a turn in the road, a new path, a BC and AD in our lives." Jesus was offering this woman a new path: You can go a new way—one that leads to life. Choose it.

Novelist Jan Karon of the famous Mitford novels, centered on a parish minister in a North Carolina mountain town, has a character say, "Every saint has a past . . . and every sinner has a future."[10]

Jesus is giving us a future. He is giving us *all* a future.

NOTES

1. Mary Gordon, *Reading Jesus: A Writer's Encounter with the Gospels* (New York: Anchor Books, 2010).

2. Gordon, 77.

3. Gordon.

4. Gordon, 78.

5. See Maggie Fazeli Ford, *The Washington Post,* March 2, 2012.

6. Gordon, 80.

7. Dorothy Sayers, "The Other Six Deadly Sins," *Creed and Chaos* (New York: Harcourt, Brace, 1949), 63.

8. Richard Rohr, from a lecture delivered at Myers Park Baptist Church, Charlotte, NC, April 2012.

9. Reynolds Price, *Three Gospels* (New York: Scribner, 1996), 33.

10. Jan Karon, *Light from Heaven* (New York: Penguin, 2006).

Chapter 6

JESUS AND
the Bent-Over Woman

The Man in the Dungeon and Me
(Luke 13:10-17)

Jesus was teaching in the synagogue, announcing the nearness of the kingdom, that very nearness present in him as healing, deliverance, justice, and joy. His kingdom was shaking the religious establishment who believed in the kingdom but wanted to be in charge of its coming. Their anthem was:

> Thy kingdom come, Thy will be done
> As long as I'm in charge (cha-a-a-arge).
> (Sing to the tune of "A Mighty Fortress.")

The Meeting

In came a woman for the Shabbat service. She was bent over and had been for eighteen years, probably a good portion of her adult life. What had bent her over? The text says literally "a spirit of weakness," *pneuma astheneia*.

Many things can bend us over. The Psalms often speak of a "crushed spirit" or "downcast heart," as in Psalm 34:18: "The LORD is near to the brokenhearted, and saves the crushed in spirit." Proverbs adds its wisdom: "A cheerful heart is a good medicine, but a downcast spirit dries up the bones" (17:22, RSV). Some days laughter is God's gift. "Another secret," writes Anne Lamott, "is that laughter is carbonated holiness."[1]

This woman's bones had dried up. Her world was cripplingly small; her eyes took in the ground; her breathing was constricted. She had been bent over for so long that her condition had become her "normal." Sometimes the abnormal has become our normal, and we can see no further than the confines of our condition. We can be bent over for physical reasons: scoliosis, osteoporosis, back injury. But we can also be bent over psychologically and spiritually—crushed in spirit with a downcast heart.

Later in the text, Jesus identifies the source of the spirit of weakness in the woman: Satan has bound her. Some of you may squirm. Satan is not in your spiritual or theological lexicon. Literally, Satan, or "the Satan," as it is always in Hebrew Scripture, means "the Accuser." The Accuser has bent her over for eighteen years.

I think I know that Satan. I see it all the time. Some days I'm that Bent-Over Woman.

The Accuser says, "You are not worthy. You'll never amount to anything. You should be ashamed. You are a disappointment." He turns "I've done something wrong" into "There's something wrong with me." He turns "You've made a mistake" into "You are a mistake." The Accuser attacks us at the level of our being, our personhood. The Accuser traffics in diminishment and in toxic shame.

Many things can bend us over: trauma from the past, grief, shame, depression, wartime trauma. Poverty can do it, or society's view of the color of our skin, or the shape of our bodies. We can internalize cultural condemnation. We feel lesser, and we feel bound. Sometimes our parents have passed on to us what had been passed to them, a spirit of accusation, passing on, often unconsciously, shame or guilt. Sometimes the church does it, meaning to be Christ but turning into the Accuser.

So we need deliverance from this spirit that cripples us. And we need to forgive family and church who did not know what they were doing, at least not fully so. And we need forgiveness for ourselves, for we did not cause this or deserve this, and we've done the best we knew to do in the face of this spirit and its crippling power.

Jesus saw the bent-over woman and approached her. She did not approach him. She did not ask for healing. Sometimes we've given up hope. We've stopped asking. But here Jesus took the initiative. And there's no mention of the woman's faith. If faith was involved in her healing, Jesus brought that too. He laid his hands on her body and said:

> "Woman, you are set free [literally, loosed] from your ailment," your *astheneia,* your infirmity." . . . Immediately she stood up straight and began praising God. (Luke 13:12-13)

Charles Wesley expresses something of what she must have felt in his hymn "O for a Thousand Tongues to Sing":

> He speaks, and listening to His voice,
> New life, the dead receive.
> The mournful, broken hearts rejoice,
> The humble poor believe.[2]

The Confrontation

Now we observe the testy little skirmish between Jesus and the local religious leaders. This is not a verbatim report. It may reflect Luke's situation where church and synagogue were in the middle of a nasty divorce. We must not read into this text an anti-Judaism that has been the terrible legacy of the church. Rather, we should see it as another dreary example of how religious leaders, now as then, become barriers to the very grace they preach. We see it today. We see a church captive to its culture and bound by its legalisms and bigotries. Then there is the "church beneath the church" alive with the compassion and Spirit of Christ. Just like the Alcoholics Anonymous meetings housed all over the country in church basements, so filled with honesty and humility, gratitude and compassion, while often above in the sanctuaries people come with their highly defended selves, running from their weaknesses and quick to judge. In the church there are the judgers and the praisers. We can't be both, at least not at the same time. We can't be praising God and judging others at the same moment.

The leader of the synagogue became indignant because Jesus healed this woman on the Sabbath, and so this religious leader said to the crowd:

> "There are six days on which work ought to be done; come on those days and be cured, and not on the sabbath day."
> (13:14)

Amy-Jill Levine, Jewish professor of New Testament at Vanderbilt, says that scholars and churches must stop the practice of trying to make Jesus look good by making Jews look bad.[3] There would have been those Jews in Jesus' day who would have condemned a healing on the Sabbath, but there were others who would have argued that a healing is the work of God, not our work, so if healing happens, praise be to God.

So Jesus argued using a good, time-tested rabbinic form of argument, from lesser to greater: You loose your animals to drink on the Sabbath. Why shouldn't God loose one of God's own children from the binding of Satan on God's Sabbath of joy and rest? And Jesus named the woman "daughter of Abraham." It is the only time in the Gospels a woman is named so, a title of highest spiritual worth.

Luke observed that with Jesus' words the religious leaders were "put to shame" (13:17). A better translation might be "were put in their place." Their hearts were exposed. And the crowd—"the entire crowd was rejoicing at all the wonderful things that he was doing" (verse 17). Again Charles Wesley's hymn reflects their joy:

O for a thousand tongues to sing
My great Redeemer's praise,
The glories of my God and King,
The triumphs of His grace.

The Man in the Dungeon

And now the man in the dungeon. Luke often paired parables and stories, one featuring a man, the other a woman. Twin stories. For example, the parables of the shepherd who lost one of his sheep, and the woman with the lost coin. Luke follows the deliverance of the bent-over woman on the Sabbath in chapter 13 with the story of a man healed of his swollen arms and legs on the Sabbath in chapter 14. I'm going to substitute another story, the man in the dungeon. Who is this man? Surely me, perhaps you. The image and the story come from the life of Frederick Buechner.

Buechner writes of going to the oldest part of the Tower of London, built by William the Conqueror in the eleventh century. It is called the White Tower. On the top floor is a beautiful small Norman chapel called the Chapel of Saint John. This is how he describes it: "It is very bare and simple . . . built all of stone with twelve stone pillars and a vaulted ceiling. There is a cool, silvery light that comes in through the arched windows. . . . The chapel is very silent, very still. . . . You cannot enter it without being struck by the feeling of purity and peace it gives. If there is any such thing in the world, it is a holy place."[4] Have you been to such a place? To a cathedral or church or place in nature that gives you a feeling of purity and peace?

But down below the chapel is the most terrible of dungeons. Its heavy oak door "locks out all light and ventilation." The room measures four feet square and four feet high. The prisoner could not stand up fully or lie down at full length. "There is," he says, "almost no air to breathe in it, almost no room to move. It is known as the Little Ease."[5]

We are the White Tower with a chapel and a dungeon. Some days we dwell in Saint John's Chapel, and other days in the Little Ease. Buechner tells of a particular period in his life when he was a prisoner in the Little Ease. His daughter was near death, slowly starving herself to death with anorexia. Her illness became his own and revealed his own. If she on one day had a piece of toast, he was "in seventh heaven." If she refused to eat, he was in hell. He writes:

> I choose the term *hell* with some care. Hell is where there is no light but only darkness, and I was so caught up in my fear for her life, which had become in a way my life too, that none of the usual sources of light worked any more, and light was what I was starving for. . . . During my daughter's sickness and its aftermath I began to realize how much of my time I spent in that dark, airless, crippling place where there was no ease at all.[6]

As Buechner's daughter got better, he "ironically or providentially" began to recognize how unwell he was. He went to twelve-step groups, had psychotherapy, dealt with his deep childhood fears, which stemmed in large part from his father's suicide when he was a boy. Experiencing his own wellness took awhile. He writes, "But the one place where I did not look to find God's presence because I'm not sure I even knew such a place existed was that Chapel of Saint John within us all where the deepest truth of who we are keeps vigil, that still, silent place where there is forgiveness and healing and hope."[7]

I have spent too many hours, too many days, below in the dungeon of the Little Ease. But I know that light-filled Chapel of Saint John exists within. Christ has led me there and still leads me there when I let him.

How would you describe your own chapel? Your place of cool, healing, silvery light? Perhaps it is a place with high vaulted ceilings that make you stand up straight or twirl around, as I once saw a child do when she entered a beautiful sanctuary. Where you breathe freely and deeply of fresh new air. Where peace and relief and joy happen in you.

My Story

On July 20, 1969, I had a car accident that changed my life. As a young college student on the way to preach, I hit a young girl who jumped suddenly into the path of my car and ended her life. I can still feel in my body the physical impact of hitting her, her body hitting the fender, then hood, then windshield of my car. Three blows that ended her life. There are moments, even today, when the horror sweeps over me.

I remember the screams of her sister, filling out the police forms, the trip in a car to meet the parents, where I sobbed out, "I'm sorry, I'm so sorry," and where they in inexplicable grace hugged me and tried to comfort *me* of all people, the three of us hugging and hanging on for dear life.

I also remember saying to myself that day, "Lord, do not let this pass too easily," a prayer that was also a kind of curse, a judgment and sentence that would haunt my life. God and the girl's parents offered grace. I became my own judge and jury. I can only imagine the grief her parents and sister have experienced. I think of them and pray for them and for the young girl still.

What I've experienced has been outsized grief and outsized guilt that have kept me too many days a prisoner in the Little Ease and has affected my life and those close to me in ways I'm still trying to understand.

But I have also had extraordinary moments in my own Chapel of Saint John with its cool, silvery light and vaulted ceilings, and breathed the fresh air of God's grace and peace.

This may be one of the reasons I love cathedrals and chapels and sanctuaries and holy places: they help lead me there, to the Chapel of Saint John within.

Sometimes I have felt the hands of Jesus on me and heard him say, "You are set free. You can leave the dungeon and enter the chapel of light." Sometimes I think he's said, "Okay, enough already. Leave that place!" And I think, I trust, that I am dwelling more and more in the Chapel of Saint John.

I know you've had your own dungeons and suffered events that have put you there. I need not name them. You have named them. Named them over and over. Perhaps you have despaired some days of escaping the dungeon and entering the Chapel of Saint John within.

But here Christ comes, as he came to that woman bent by life, taking initiative, not waiting for us to ask, not demanding some kind of faith, but bringing it, laying his hands on us, straightening us up, and leading us up and out, or deep within, to the light.

Praise God, and Christ, and Holy Spirit!

NOTES

1. Anne Lamott, *Plan B: Further Thoughts on Faith* (NY: Riverhead Books, 2005), 66.

2. Charles Wesley, "O For a Thousand Tongues to Sing," 1739.

3. Amy-Jill Levine, *The Misunderstood Jew: The Church and the Scandal of the Jewish Jesus* (New York: HarperSanFrancisco, 2006).

4. Frederick Buechner, *Telling Secrets* (New York: HarperSanFrancisco, 1991), 46.

5. Buechner.

6. Buechner, 25, 46.

7. Buechner, 51–52.

Chapter 7

JESUS AND the Rich Young Ruler and Zacchaeus

Money, Possessions, and Us
(Mark 10:17-27; Luke 19:1-10)

Someone has said that Jesus talked more about money than any other subject except the kingdom of God, which was the underlying theme of all that he taught. You may now be holding your pocketbooks a little tighter—when Jesus wants us to hold them a little lighter.

The Sermon on the Mount sets the tone:

> "Do not store up for yourselves treasures on earth where moth and rust consume and where thieves break in and steal; but store up for yourselves treasures in heaven. . . . For where your treasure is, there your heart will be also. . . . No one can serve two masters; for a slave will either hate the one and love the other, or be devoted to one and despise the other. You cannot serve God and wealth." (Matthew 6:19-21,24)

All three Synoptic Gospels—Matthew, Mark, and Luke—record this vivid saying of Jesus:

"It is easier for a camel to go through the eye of a needle than for someone who is rich to enter the kingdom of God." (10:25)

"Yikes!" we exclaim, clutching our pocketbooks even more tightly.

I offer two contrasting encounters with Jesus that concern our relationship with wealth: the man often called "the rich young ruler" and Zacchaeus the tax collector.

The Encounter

The story of the rich young ruler was so important to the early church that all three Synoptic Gospels record it. I shall use Mark's telling of the story.

A man ran up to Jesus and knelt before him and asked,

"Good Teacher, what must I do to inherit eternal life?" (10:17)

Matthew calls him a young man, and Luke calls him a ruler, hence the normal description of him as the rich young ruler. We can sense his eagerness and earnestness.

"What must I do to be saved?" we ask. It is the fundamental question. The man must have been strongly drawn to Jesus. He ran to him and knelt, an act of worship. But as we shall see, it is easier to worship Jesus than to follow him.

"Good Teacher," answered the young man surprisingly:

"Why do you call me good? No one is good but God alone." (10:18)

Jesus' humility here surprises us. He did not presume Godlike perfection in goodness.

What must we do to inherit eternal life? Jesus had more in mind than getting us into heaven, though life forever with God, in God, was part of what he meant. However, what he had in mind was becoming part of God's life, God's way, starting now.

Jesus answered the man's question like this:

> "You know the commandments: 'You shall not murder; You shall not commit adultery; You shall not steal; You shall not bear false witness; You shall not defraud; Honor your father and your mother.'" (10:19)

The man answered,

> "Teacher, I have kept all these since my youth." (10:20)

"Then Jesus, looking at him, loved him"—loved him, the text says—and said,

> "You lack one thing; go, sell what you own, and give the money to the poor, and you will have treasure in heaven; then come follow me." (10:21)

"Go ... sell ... give ... follow." Those were the stirring commands of Jesus to this man. Mark records this man's response:

> At that saying his countenance fell, and he went away sorrowful; for he had great possessions. (10:22, RSV)

We are sad along with the man. We want eternal life for him.

Here is one of those unusual encounters in the Gospels when a person wants to follow Jesus but decides not to because of the demands of following.

"Go ... sell ... give ... follow." There are many throughout Christian history who have heard these words and followed. Saint Francis did—along with his followers up to us today. The first Scripture verse in the Franciscan Rule is this verse. And we think of Mother Teresa living among the poor of Calcutta and Dorothy Day working among the poor in New York City.

This man had it all—youth, power, money, and a good, moral life—but he could not let go of his wealth.

Jesus and the Disciples

The scene shifts to Jesus and the disciples. Jesus commented,

"How hard it will be for those who have wealth to enter the kingdom of God!" (10:23)

And now the riveting saying:

"It is easier for a camel to go through the eye of a needle than for a rich man to enter the kingdom of God." (10:25, RSV)

The disciples caught the hardness of this saying and asked,

"Then who can be saved?" (10:26)

Jesus answered,

"For mortals it is impossible, but not for God; for God all things are possible." (10:27)

Letting go of our attachment to wealth to follow Jesus requires a work of grace in our hearts. Did Jesus know that this man had such an attachment to his wealth that he needed to let go of his wealth and give it to the poor before he could inherit eternal life? Was this the concrete way *this* man could love God with all his heart, mind, soul, and strength and love his neighbor as himself?

The Story and Us

Some scholars have tried to wriggle out of the hard demands of Jesus' saying "It is easier for a camel to go through the eye of a needle than for a rich man to enter the kingdom of God." Some claim that the word *camel* is very close in the Greek to the word for "rope." Jesus must have meant "rope." So it is hard but not impossible for a rope to go through the eye of a needle.

Others suggest that there was a very small gate in Jerusalem called the "Needle's Eye." A camel had to squeeze to get through. If it was carrying cargo, it couldn't; but if it was unburdened, it could. Jesus must be rolling his eyes.

These interpretations ruin the intentional hyperbole of Jesus' saying and make nonsense of the disciples' response: "Then who can be saved?" Jesus' words were clear: it is impossible to enter the kingdom when you are in thrall to your riches.

Another way of softening this command, "Go . . . sell . . . give . . . follow," is to say that this command belongs to a special category of followers—like monastics who take the vow of poverty. But this lets all the rest of us off the hook from examining our relationship to our wealth.

We should be left with the sharp demand of Jesus: that the man go and sell and give to the poor in order to follow him and inherit eternal life. And with the man's response: his going sadly away. We are saddened by this man's no to Jesus. We wished his response were different. Maybe, we hope, the man changed his mind later and sold his possessions, gave to the poor, and followed. Jesus told a parable about a man who said no then later said yes. Could this have happened to the young man? Could it happen to us?

We must take seriously the rich young ruler's response. New Testament scholar Paul Minear comments about this story: "It preserves a dominant accent in Jesus' proclamation of the Kingdom's approach: threat for the wealthy, proud, privileged, self-sufficient, righteous ones; promise for the poor, humble, dispossessed, ostracized, sinful."[1]

Jesus and Zacchaeus

Now we turn to Zacchaeus. Luke records the story of Zacchaeus in the chapter just after the story of the rich young ruler: he, rich, had turned sadly away.

Now Jesus was passing through Jericho, where Zacchaeus lived. He is described as a "chief tax collector and . . . rich" (19:2). He was triply damned: not only a tax collector but a chief tax collector, and not only a chief tax collector but rich. Tax collectors were regarded as traitors by the Jews for their service to Rome and as cheats because they had the unregulated power to gouge the people for as much money as they could and keep the extra for themselves. A rich tax collector was good at gouging.

Zacchaeus had heard that Jesus was coming to Jericho. What happened is the surprise of mercy, or to use Flannery O'Connor's notion, "the shock of grace."[2] Zacchaeus went to find Jesus and discovered that Jesus was in search of him. An old hymn by an unknown lyricist describes what Zacchaeus experienced:

> I sought the Lord, and afterward I knew
> He moved my soul to seek him, seeking me;
> It was not I that found, O Savior true.
> No, I was found, was found of Thee.

The One we are looking for is looking for us.

When Zacchaeus got to the street where Jesus was coming, the crowd blocked his view because he was very short. Picture Danny DeVito in a robe. Fighting back his inclination to retreat, to curse his height or the crowd, he became as a child, scampered up a sycamore tree, and unwittingly readied himself to greet the kingdom of God.

Jesus was inviting himself to dinner at Zacchaeus's house as an act, when he spied him up in the tree and said,

> "Zacchaeus, hurry and come down; for I must stay at your house today." (19:5)

Jesus was inviting himself to dinner as an act of divine friendship.

You could have heard a pin drop; then came the grumbling of the crowd:

"He has gone in to be the guest of one who is a sinner."
(19:7)

Ugly spirituality.

When Jesus and Zacchaeus were eating dinner, Zacchaeus
suddenly stood and up and said,

> "Look, half of my possessions, Lord [Jesus had become his
> Lord], I will give to the poor; and if I have defrauded anyone
> of anything, I will pay back four times as much." (19:8)

His servants probably fainted on the spot.

This was conversion in the Hebrew sense of the word: an
about-face. It was repentance in the New Testament sense of
the word, the changing of one's mind. Zacchaeus was given
a new mind.

The salvation Jesus brings moves us from the calculus
of the law to the extravagance of grace. The Jewish law
encouraged you to give no more than 20 percent to the poor,
and thieves were to make from simple to double restitu-
tion.[3] Zacchaeus went far beyond the requirements of law.
"Today," Jesus said, "salvation has come to this house."
Then he called this converted traitor and cheat a "son of
Abraham" (19:9).

This was an astonishing moment. Social gospel theologian
Walter Rauschenbusch commented, "Here a camel passed
through the needle's eye, and Jesus stood and cheered."[4]
Here is the divine comedy at work—a scoundrel becomes
the hero of the story, all because of the transformative power
of the divine friendship embodied in Jesus. Impossible? What
is impossible for us is possible with God.

The contrasts of these stories catch one's attention. The
rich young ruler came running to Jesus and went away sad.
Zacchaeus waited up in a tree, and at the end of the story he
is clothed in joy. One said no; the other said yes.

If you try to use the logic of the law, what took place in
these encounters does not make sense. Jesus demanded all

the wealth of the rich young ruler. Zacchaeus got off with half (plus the extravagant reparations)! Jesus is not legalistic about our relationship to our wealth; he comes with freedom in his hand and the offer of a new way of living.

Jesus' command to us all is in some real measure to let go of our attachment to wealth, to go, sell, give to the poor, and come and follow. We each have to decide what this means in our lives. It means something, some letting go of wealth and giving to the poor. The early church gave of their private property so that the poor among them would be helped. Later the giving of alms became part of weekly worship.

It is important for the interpreter not to stand between the text and the hearer of the text, making the text too hard or too easy. Our goal is to stand before Jesus, hear his voice, and follow.

Dietrich Bonhoeffer is often quoted as saying that the commandment of Christ is never in abstract, always concrete. Christ speaks into the circumstances of our lives and bids us to follow. The stories of the rich young ruler and Zacchaeus train our ears to listen.

NOTES

1. Paul Minear, *Commands of Christ* (New York: Abingdon, 1972), 110.

2. See "Flannery O'Connor: The Shock of Grace," Lay Centre at Forer Unitas, November 17, 2014, http://www.laycentre .org/schede-95-flannery_oconnor_the_shock_of_grace, accessed December 17, 2018.

3. See Exodus 22:1-15, and various writings on the mitzvah of tzedakah.

4. Walter Rauschenbusch, *The Social Principles of Jesus* (New York: Association Press, 1921), 68.

Chapter 8

JESUS AND the Blind Man

A Two-Stage Healing and the Journey toward Wholeness (Mark 8:22-26)

I was originally drawn to Jesus' encounter with the blind man because it is the only time the Gospels record Jesus healing someone in stages. Or we could put it this way: it is the only healing miracle that took Jesus two tries.

But this miracle in stages gave me an odd hope: maybe there's hope for me yet! For *us* yet. Some things take a lot longer to heal than others—I'm speaking of body *and* mind here. A cut on the skin can heal almost overnight. Some mental traumas can take years to heal.

A few years ago, I flipped a golf cart on top of me. My left leg was hurt most badly. My leg—variously crunched, burned, punctured, and skinned—took about three months to heal. I was ready for it to be healed much sooner! But now I look upon it as my slow-motion miracle. I look at my leg, now fully functioning with funny-looking scars, and say, "I thank you, God." There's a parable in there somewhere.

Wholeness, Healing, and Cure

This text helps us probe the distinction between a cure and a healing, and between healing and wholeness. You can be cured of an illness but not be healed in any deeper sense of your being. Or even though you may not be cured, you may nevertheless experience a deeper kind of healing.

I knew a woman who was battling cancer and in the last months of her life. One day she exclaimed to her daughter, "I've been healed." She did not mean "cured" but a deeper spiritual healing readying her for death and eternal life.

We all seek a wholeness that goes beyond any particular cure or healing. We all are on a journey toward the kind of healing we call wholeness. You might describe it as a oneness with God, self, and life itself. We may experience this wholeness of body, mind, and spirit here and there, now and then—it's a miracle when we do—but we don't have it fully and not always, at every moment. We are on a journey toward it.

In British novelist Susan Howatch's novel *The Heartbreaker*, there is a healing ministry founded by a church called St. Benet's Healing Center. In this ministry they make a distinction between a healing and a cure. Here is how they say it: "A complete cure can never be guaranteed, but a healing, an improvement in the quality of life, is always possible. One should think of health as a journey towards a cure, a journey punctuated by healings." One of the characters comments, "And anyway, one can argue that a complete cure is never possible because no one can be completely well in mind, body and spirit—it is the journey towards the cure that is so vital."[1] Does this sound hopeful or discouraging to you? At the time it felt hopeful to me.

I was rummaging around the Union Theological Seminary library a few summers ago and thumbing through a book by Jungian analyst and professor of religion and psychology at Union, Ann Belford Ulanov. I was arrested by a passage in which she said that pop psychology promises too much: buy this tape, read this book—and be whole! She says the great spiritual traditions of the world—Christianity, Judaism, Islam, Buddhism—offer a deeper wisdom: "Spiritual traditions instruct us that we are never whole. We are the sinners, the ones living in bondage in Egypt, disobedient to Allah's will, mixed up in the ten-thousand things. But even in that condition we are loved while yet sinners, Yahweh calls us into an exodus from oppression, Allah calls us to daily prayer and the Bodhisattva refrains from bliss until each of us can attain it too."[2]

There it is. We may be sinners, but God has not given up on us. God loves us even there. We may still be in bondage, but God still comes to deliver. Exodus is forever. We may be caught in the ten thousand things, as Buddhism puts it, but God is there with us moving us toward wholeness. In the Buddhist tradition the Buddhist saint, the Bodhisattva, attains enlightenment and gets to the gates of Nirvana but, instead of entering, turns back to the world to help others get there, like a shepherd going after a lost sheep; like Jesus.

In his prose poem "*Hagia Sophia*" (Holy Wisdom), Thomas Merton wrote, "There is in all visible things an invisible fecundity . . . a hidden wholeness."[3] The phrase "hidden wholeness" stirs up hope in me. It is there, like an underground stream, in our original self, the true self created in the divine image. We can draw upon its waters. We can excavate through the layers of false self to get to our authentic true self. We can be a pilgrim there, on the journey toward wholeness—and even experience it while on our way there.

The word *salvation* means healing and wholeness. We can speak of it as the discovery that life can be lived, that we can "*live full out,* with all our heart, mind, soul and strength," as Ann Ulanov puts it.[4] We can do this, whatever our physical condition, or how much we have lost. As Jesus said, "Those who find their life will lose it, and those who lose their life for my sake will find it" (Matthew 10:39), or as blind musician and composer Ken Medema sings, "Finding leads to losing and losing lets you find."[5]

The apostle Paul prayed to God to be delivered of what he called his "thorn in the flesh." We do not know what it was, but it must have been a painful and humiliating, and in some measure crippling, infirmity of body or mind. He prayed fervently, desperately, repeatedly for a healing, but the healing did not come. Instead, what he got was this word from God: "My grace is sufficient for you; for power is made perfect in weakness" (2 Corinthians 12:9). The answer? Not a deliverance from his infirmity but a grace sufficient for his life in his journey toward wholeness. By that sufficient grace he would live. The words in the hymn "How Firm a Foundation" express the concept well:

When through fiery trials thy pathway shall lie,

My grace, all-sufficient, shall be thy supply.

Sometimes we may not receive the cure we want, but grace all-sufficient shall be our supply on our journey toward wholeness.

The Healing

Now to the Gospel text in Mark. Jesus and his disciples had come to the village of Bethsaida. Some of the villagers brought a blind man to Jesus and begged Jesus to touch him and heal him. Please, Jesus, touch and heal my friend, my child, my spouse, my sister, my brother, *me*.

Sometimes it takes a village to be healed, a community of friends. We cannot necessarily get to Jesus on our own. We cannot necessarily get to wholeness from here. So here comes the church, here comes Alcoholics Anonymous, here come some friends. They take us to be healed.

But then the text says that Jesus took the man by the hand and led him out of the village. Why this? Perhaps Jesus knew that while we all need community in the healing process, in the project called wholeness, healing finally, fully happens in that place where we and God go alone together. It's us and Jesus, nobody else in this sanctuary of the heart. Sometimes we need to get away from the voices in our heads or the voices of the community to be able to hear Jesus' voice.

Jesus now got very, shall we say, physical, as physical as spit. He spat in his hands and anointed the man's eyes. This act involved an exchange of body fluids, not as contamination but as healing.

Sometimes healing gets that close, that messy, that risky. It is a metaphor of incarnation, God getting that close, that messy, that risky in Jesus.

Jesus then asked,

"Can you see anything?" (8:23)

The man replied,

"I can see people, but they look like trees, walking." (8:24)

Jesus was undeterred by the incompleteness of the miracle. He repeated the process—laying his hands on the man's eyes again. This time the text says,

[The man] looked intently and his sight was restored, and he saw everything clearly. (8:25)

Jesus never gives up. And so we never give up. Don't let discouragement cause you to quit the road to wholeness. As Winston Churchill said, "Never give in. Never give in. Never, never, never, never." Six *nevers*!

Then Jesus told the man not to reenter the village. *Why?* we wonder. Perhaps the village would not accept his healing. They were used to blind old Joe, not ready for the new Joe.

(In family systems theory, the family may not want the ill family member, the "identified patient," to get well because it will involve changes in the family.) Sometimes we ourselves have gotten so comfortable in our illness, our lack of wholeness, that we are not ready to step out into the new. Jesus asked a man in one healing encounter, "Do you want to be made well?" (John 5:6, RSV; see chapter 3). Sometimes we're not ready; other times our community is not ready. We have to get well together. Maybe Jesus knew that the village was not ready.

Or perhaps Jesus' instruction was more in line with what he often told people whom he healed: "Do not tell anyone. Keep it quiet!" Why this? Perhaps because he knew his mission was greater than physical healing—as important as that is! He was after a deeper healing, a healing that is wholeness, a reconciliation with God and self and life itself.

Remember these words of Jesus: "I came that they may have life, and have it abundantly. . . . Peace I leave with you; my peace I give to you. I do not give to you as the world gives. . . . I have said these things to you so that my joy may be in you, and that your joy may be complete" (John 10:10; 14:27; 15:11). Life, peace, joy. Jesus' words suggest a wholeness and fullness of life not dependent on our physical condition or our investment account. People I've known who have achieved this kind of wholeness, contentment, peace, and joy have often been people who have met much adversity and suffered cruel turns of fate. It's almost as if calamity has opened a new door to them. Jesus' mission was a deeper healing.

Spiritual Blindness and Sightedness

I think Mark wants us to see this healing of the blind man as a parable of regaining our spiritual sightedness. Here is a miracle we need every day. Spiritual blindness afflicts us all.

Just before this healing encounter, Jesus confronted his disciples about their spiritual blindness. They had just seen

Jesus feed four thousand people with seven loaves and a few small fish, and now they were in a veritable twit over having only one loaf. Jesus said to them, "Why are you talking about having no bread? Do you still not perceive or understand? . . . Do you have eyes, and fail to see? Do you have ears, and fail to hear?" (Mark 8:17-18). A little tough love here. A little earlier, in Mark 7:32-35, Jesus had healed a deaf man with a speech impediment. He had put his fingers in the man's ears and spat and touched the man's tongue. Then he looked to the heavens and said "*Ephphatha!*" which means "Be opened!" And the man's ears were opened. Now Jesus said to his disciples, "You have perfectly good ears; can you not hear? You have two good eyes, can you not see? Do you not yet understand?"

The healings of blind people in the Gospels can become parables of opening spiritually blind eyes. On our journey toward wholeness, we need to open our eyes to all God is doing and has done. As someone has said, "There is no lack of wonders, only a lack of wonderment." The poet E. E. Cummings wrote a poem about the beauty of one fine day: "i thank You God for most this amazing day," and ends the poem with "Now the ears of my ears awake and / now the eyes of my eyes are opened."[6]

The apostle Paul spoke of having "the eyes of your heart enlightened" (Ephesians 1:18). Don't we all hope for this miracle, to have the eyes of our hearts opened to all God is doing? Gratitude is a new way of seeing. It is our home in God's presence. Richard Rohr spoke of moving from "dual thinking," us-versus-them thinking, to "unitive thinking" where we see all of life as one in the oneness of God.[7] In a Peter Mayer song, the lyricist now sees all life as a miracle, and "everything is holy now."

Jesus comes to bring us "second sight," not just physical seeing but spiritual seeing. Jamake Hightower, a Blackfoot Indian, writes of the Native American experience called "looking twice." First we look at the physical world, "bring our eyes together in front" and see the glistening dew on the grass, a clear running stream, the dazzling blue of a bluebird in flight. But then comes a second looking, "on the edge of what is visible," to the spiritual realm. He says, "You must learn to look at the world twice if you want to see all there is to see."[8] Sometimes Jesus says, "Open your eyes." Other times he says, "Open your eyes *again!*"

This two-stage miracle suggests that we are on the path toward wholeness. Paul used the verb for salvation in three tenses: we have been saved, we shall be saved, and we are being saved.

Poet Maya Angelou says that when a person comes up to her and announces, "I'm a Christian!" she replies, "Already?!" We are on a journey of faith toward being who God made us and is calling us to be. This applies to the church too. We are, as I once heard David Buttrick say, "the assuredly-broken-yet-being-saved" body of Christ. We are traveling toward wholeness together.

There may be a miracle out there. As people in Alcoholics Anonymous say, "Don't leave before a miracle happens." And as Mary Chapin Carpenter sings in her song, "The Age of Miracles," "There's one on the way."

NOTES

1. Susan Howatch, *The Heartbreaker* (New York: Alfred A. Knopf, 2004), 462.

2. Ann Belford Ulanov, *Spiritual Aspects of Clinical Work* (Einsiedeln, Switzerland: Daimon Verlag, 2006), 20.

3. Thomas Merton, "Hagia Sophia," in *A Thomas Merton Reader*, ed. Thomas McDonnell (New York: Image/Doubleday, 1974, 1989), 506.

4. Ann Belford Ulanov, *The Unshuttered Heart* (Nashville: Abingdon Press, 2007), 1.

5. Ken Medema, as heard in concert and repeated on his blog, Medemasong.

6. E. E. Cummings, "i thank You God for most this amazing," *100 Selected Poems* (New York: Grove Press, 1954), 114.

7. Richard Rohr, from a lecture delivered at Myers Park Baptist Church, Charlotte, NC, April 27, 2012.

8. Jamake Hightower, quoted in Barbara Brown Taylor, *The Preaching Life* (Cambridge: Cowley, 1993), 45.

Chapter 9

JESUS AND
Blind Bartimaeus

The Gospel as Healing
(Mark 10:46-52)

The story of Jesus' encounter with Bartimaeus is drenched in joy. It is a cameo of Jesus' healing ministry, the gospel in a glance. Let's slow down and take a look. We may find more than we expect to see.

Setting the Stage

Jesus and his disciples were on their way to Jerusalem and the last days of Jesus' life. The crowd following him grew larger the closer they got to the City of David. Jesus had come to Jericho, a town about fifteen miles from Jerusalem. As he was leaving the city by the road to Jerusalem, he was flanked by the disciples and a "large crowd" (10:46). Evidently, as Jesus traveled from Galilee to Jerusalem more and more people joined.

By the side of the road sat a blind beggar named Bartimaeus. He must have heard by the buzz of the crowd who was about to pass by. The man began to cry out,

"Jesus, Son of David, have mercy on me!" (10:47)

This man's cry is the basis of the most famous prayer in Eastern Orthodox spirituality, the Jesus Prayer: "Lord Jesus

Christ, Son of God, have mercy on me, a sinner."[1] Also called The Prayer of the Heart, the Jesus Prayer is to be prayed all through the day until it becomes as the beating of one's heart. The man's cry is echoed in the Kyrie sung by millions of Christians every Sunday: "Lord have mercy, Christ have mercy, Lord have mercy."

The Crowd's Response

The crowd, however, had no interest in this man's need: "Many sternly ordered him to be quiet" (10:48). "Shut up." Had they grown tired of the man's incessant neediness? Had they grown blind to him? We know what it is to become blind to the poor around us. Then one breaks through our trained obliviousness with his or her hand out. We think, *Go away*. In contrast, Mother Teresa of Calcutta would say of the poor who came for help: "here comes Christ in another distressing disguise."

At Broadway Baptist Church in Fort Worth, Texas, a center-city church, we held an "agape meal" for the homeless community every Thursday. It was a delicious meal served family-style by the members of the church. For an hour or so every Thursday afternoon we could see homeless people walking toward the church from north, south, east, and west. On average, 150 to 200 came to the meal. The Southside Development Corporation expressed their dislike of our assembling such a large number of homeless people in the area of the city they were trying to develop. Sometimes we do not like the cry of the poor at our doorstep.

Undeterred by the crowd's shushing of him, the blind man cried out even more loudly, "Jesus, Son of David, have mercy on me." I remember the signs that Memphis garbage workers on strike wore in the days before Martin Luther King Jr. was assassinated: "I Am a Man" they said. Theirs was a cry to be acknowledged as human beings deserving respect. Today signs say "Black Lives Matter." As we shall see, *sick* lives matter too.

Jesus' Response

The story turns with the next three words: "Jesus stood still" (10:49). He was headed somewhere, to his appointment with the powers that be in Jerusalem, but he stopped. When Moses passed by the burning bush in the desert, he could have kept right on going, but the text says that he "turn[ed] aside" (Exodus 3:3) to see what was going on. And out of that burning bush, God called Moses to free the Hebrew people from slavery under Pharaoh. Sometimes we need to stop and pay attention to what is going on around us. Jesus stood still, Moses turned aside, and life was changed.

Then Jesus moved into action. "Call him," he said to his disciples.

The disciples did and said to the man words that thrill me because they are at the heart of the church's evangelical message:

"Take heart; get up, he is calling you." (10:49, RSV)

What more joyful words can we, the church, say to a person? *Evangelical*: from the Greek *euangelion*, "good news, gospel." What gladness is in these words: "Take heart; get up, he is calling you."

Evangelism is answering Jesus' words, "Call him here" (10:49). It is bringing people into the vicinity of Christ where good things can happen. We point not to ourselves but to Christ. As Paul put it, "What we preach is not ourselves, but Jesus Christ as Lord" (2 Corinthians 4:5, RSV). We do so with our actions as well as our words. As a quote popularly attributed to Saint Francis goes, "Preach the gospel everywhere. If necessary, use words." There are hurting people in this world, and there is Christ. We are called to bring them together.

I mentioned above the agape meal at Broadway Baptist Church. After we sat together at the meal, we would invite people to stay for a short worship service. About half the people stayed. One homeless person told me about our not requiring worship attendance before the meal: "Thanks for giving us our freedom of religion." After worship we invited anyone who wanted communion to meet in the chapel next door. About twenty or so would ordinarily come. Most had not had communion since they had become homeless.

There was a transsexual woman who began to come to the meal. After a few months she began to stay for the worship. Then one night she came for communion. When she met me at the communion table, she said, "All my life I've been told church was the last place that would accept me. I have never in my life felt so accepted as here." She had heard Christ's voice in our meal together, and it felt like good news.

Sometimes we turn the Good News, *euangelion*, into bad news, *mal-angelion*. We surround the Good News with threats: Believe or judgment is coming! Or with conditions: God loves you *if*. . . . God loves you, *but*. . . . God loves you if you are good, if you believe the right way. God loves you, but you better shape up. Conditions. Yet God loves us unconditionally. No mixed messages. Jesus is the eternal Yes of God. Do not fear any hidden noes.

Paul wrote, "For the Son of God, Jesus Christ, whom we preached among you . . . was not Yes and No; but in him it is always Yes. For all the promises of God find their Yes in him" (2 Corinthians 1:19-20, RSV). The blind man heard this yes, threw off his cloak, sprang up, and came to Jesus. Was he guided by the hand? None of us come to Jesus alone; we are helped. Did he, blind, follow the sound of Jesus' voice, just as we all, blind in our own ways, follow the sound of his voice to him?

I once heard a pre-sermon prayer that I especially love, it goes like this:

O Christ, help us hear your word
and hearing your word, love your voice
and loving your voice, do your will.

We come to Christ because, hearing his word, we love his voice.

I baptized a young adult in a river one day. He asked if before I baptized him, he could recite these words of Jesus; he had come to Jesus by these words, by his voice:

> Come unto me, you that are weary and heavy laden and I will give you rest. Take my yoke upon you, and learn of me, for I am gentle and lowly in heart, and you will find rest for your souls. For my yoke is easy and my burden is light. (Matthew 11: 29-30)

The Question and the Healing

When the man got to Jesus, Jesus asked a simple but disarming question—one that calls for the deepest response we know to give. "What do you want me to do for you?" Jesus asked (10:51). We need to claim our need. Fortunate we are, blessed even, if we know our deepest need.

A compelling spiritual exercise would be to imagine Jesus coming to you and asking, "What do you want me to do for you?" It is a tender and vulnerable question. Be still with the question for a little while. How would you answer?

It's a great question for the local church to consider. What if Jesus showed up at a church's door and asked, "What do you want me to do for you?" If a church took time to answer that question, it might change a church.

The man had been begging for alms, for food, for anything that might sustain him for another day. Yet he knew his deepest need, and he went for broke:

> "My teacher, let me see again." (10:51)

O Thou who did make our eyes, mend our eyes.
Then Jesus said,

> "Go; your faith has made you well." (10:52)

77

And the man "immediately" regained his sight and "followed [Jesus] on the way" (10:52). Some whom Jesus healed he told to go back to their homes. But this man followed him on the way, and the way led to Jerusalem where Jesus would enter triumphantly on a lowly donkey, turn over tables in the temple, be arrested, tried, nailed to a cross, and die. Bartimaeus followed him "on the way," which led to the cross. Jesus told those who would follow him to count the cost. Are we willing to follow Jesus on the way, even if the cross looms?

Seeing and Living

This story, an extraordinary story about how we, blind, can gain our sight, is the last story in Mark's Gospel before Jesus entered Jerusalem.

"Your faith has made you well," Jesus said. He said it often. We may draw back anxiously and question ourselves: "Do I have enough faith to be saved, healed, made whole? [Saved, healed, and made whole are the same word in the Greek.] Surely I must need a lot of that faith!" But Jesus said that if we have faith the size of a mustard seed, it will be enough to move mountains (Matthew 17:20). That tiny—all we need to do is to crack open the door. Sometimes Jesus' very presence cracks open the door. *Take heart; get up, he is calling you!*

Did Mark include this story as the last healing story to make a point? That we all are blind, that there are many things we aren't quite seeing right, and that Jesus is saving us to a fuller, truer way of seeing and living. Charles Wesley captured the gladness of the moment when our eyes are opened in his hymn "O for a Thousand Tongues to Sing":

Hear Him, ye deaf; His praise, ye dumb,
Your loosened tongues employ;
Ye blind, behold your Savior come;
And leap, ye lame, for joy.
Our Savior comes still.

NOTES

1. A beautiful Russian Orthodox spiritual classic about this prayer is *The Way of a Pilgrim*. It tells of a man who went across Russia reciting this prayer. Earliest versions of this prayer did not include the words "a sinner," which were added later.

Chapter 10

JESUS AND the Woman Who Anointed Him at Bethany

A Time for Extravagance
(Mark 14:3-9)*

Jesus' encounter with a woman who anoints him with expensive perfume is told in two settings in the Gospels. Matthew and Mark locate the encounter at the home of Simon the leper in Bethany (Matthew 26:6-13; Mark 14:3-9), and the woman who anoints Jesus is unnamed. In John's Gospel, the encounter takes place in the home of Mary, Martha, and Lazarus in Bethany, and Mary is the one who anoints Jesus (John 12:1-8). Luke's Gospel records what I believe is another anointing, this time by a "woman in the city" in the house of a Pharisee (Luke 7:36-50). We will concentrate on Mark's account.

This beautiful domestic scene is surrounded by treachery and betrayal. Just before this scene we see the chief priests and scribes looking for a way to arrest Jesus "by stealth and

*This chapter was inspired by a sermon by Edmund Steimle preached in the early 1970s.

kill him" (14:1). "Not during the festival," they say, "or there may be a riot among the people" (14:2). Just after this scene, Judas goes to the chief priests to betray him.

Jesus was enjoying a meal in the home of Simon the leper. There must have been a story there—a healing, no doubt, and a relationship of deep gratitude. His home was in Bethany, a few miles from Jerusalem. Jesus had entered Jerusalem on a lowly donkey and turned over the tables of the money changers in the temple. The text says it was two days before Passover, so we might place the encounter on Tuesday of Holy Week. How wonderful it would be if the church reserved an evening in Holy Week between Palm Sunday and Maundy Thursday to remember this story liturgically in worship, or around dinner tables—an "Anointing Tuesday" observance.[1]

The Anointing

As Jesus and Simon and the other guests were reclining at the table for the meal, a woman came into the room with an alabaster flask of pure nard, "very costly" the text says, and poured it over Jesus' head. She emptied the entire flask of rare and expensive perfumed oil on him in an extravagant act of devotion, a sumptuous sacrifice, as saints always give sumptuously of themselves.[2] Out of love, she poured it all out, not measuring out some and saving the rest.

Why would she have done this if not in response to the lavish love of God she had seen and experienced in Jesus? Had she followed him on the edge of the crowd and watched? Or was she in the inner circle of Jesus' followers?

The Extravagant Love of God

We see the extravagant love of God in creation itself. In his poem "The Excesses of God"[3] the poet Robinson Jeffers tells of a God who went beyond the necessary to make a world full of beauty. He called it "The extravagant kindness of God." Think of the colors of flowers, brightly ribboned canyons, the beauty of the moon in the night sky, sunrise and sunset, sparkling rivers gleaming in the sun. The extravagant kindness of God indeed.

We see God's extravagant kindness, as this woman saw it, in God's act of redemption in Jesus, God's love poured out for us all on the cross. But not just on the cross—Jesus' whole life was a pouring out of himself in love. To paraphrase John's words, loving us, he loved us to the end (John 13:1). He lived and died to show a love so deep and high and wide that we will never be apart from it.

British mystic Evelyn Underhill wrote that worship is "summed up in sacrifice," the response of the human creature to the extravagant sacrifice of God in Christ and our own participation in it, however small. Such sacrifice is a "positive act," not something "given up," but "given,"[4] the way lovers give to the one they love.

This scene is in praise of immoderation for love's sake. Love itself is immoderate. Who wants to be loved moderately? Don't we all wish for something to which we can give our whole heart? This woman had experienced herself as the Beloved—as Christ wishes for us all—and was giving her whole heart, nothing held back. C. S. Lewis wrote about the anointing, "The precious alabaster box which we have to break over the holy feet is our heart."[5]

Reflecting on the fact that Jesus received this gift is startling. Our Lord not only gave sumptuously but also received sumptuously. In true encounter, we both give and receive. We are often better at giving than receiving. Here Jesus teaches us how to receive. His receiving, too, was in praise of immoderation.

The Disciples' Response

How did Jesus' disciples respond? In self-righteous indignation:

> "Why was the ointment wasted in this way? For this oint-
> ment could have been sold for more than three hundred de-
> narii, and the money given to the poor." And they scolded
> her. (14:4-5)

If the woman was lifted from arithmetic into love, they were
counting! Three hundred denarii, a year's wages. Why would
the woman "waste" the ointment?

Jesus' chosen followers were hardly ideal disciples here.
Nor are they generally portrayed as ideal disciples in the
Gospels. As New Testament scholar Ulrich Luz wrote,
"They represent Christians as they actually are—people
who have small faith (Matthew 8:26; 16:8), are ambitious
(Matthew 18:1), have an aversion to suffering (Matthew
16:22-23), doubt (Matthew 28:17), and—by no means for
the first time—are defensive toward a woman (Matthew
15:23)."[6] As the passion of Christ approached, their weaknesses would become even more apparent.

Their objection had its point. Why would the woman
consider pouring the equivalent of a year's wages over Jesus'
head? What good this money could have done for the poor!

What church serious about its discipleship does not
struggle consciously between money spent in beautiful acts
of worship and money spent on behalf of the poor? Albert
Camus captured the point: "Yes, there is beauty and there
are the humiliated. Whatever the difficulties of the under-
taking, I should like never to be unfaithful either to one or
to the other."[7]

When I was pastor at Broadway Baptist Church in Fort
Worth, Texas, we built one of the great new pipe organs in
the world at the time, at a cost of more than two million
dollars. At the same time, the church ministered daily to the

homeless community in its center-city neighborhood, including an "agape meal" that fed around two hundred homeless persons every Thursday night and offered worship and communion after the meal. We were trying, hard as it was, not to be unfaithful to beauty or to the humiliated. For a period of time, St. John the Divine Cathedral in New York City delayed the completion of its towers in order to minister more fully to the poor of the city. It was dubbed "St. John the Unfinished."[8]

Jesus commanded the rich young ruler to sell, give to the poor, and come follow him (Luke 12:33; see chapter 7). Were his words ringing in their ears as they objected? Every church has a holy struggle on its hands with those words.

Jesus' Response

What did Jesus do? He said,

"Let her alone; why do you trouble her?" (14:6)

With these three words, Jesus defended everyone who has tried to follow him only to have their way of following demeaned and dismissed. Parker Palmer says we are called to be "celebrants, advocates, defenders" of life wherever we find it.[9] Jesus became the celebrant, advocate, and defender of the woman and her gifts. Jesus declared,

"She has done a beautiful thing to me." (Mark 14:6, RSV)

Jesus' words defend the people who have offered gifts to the church but whose gifts have been refused or discarded, whose beautiful voices have been stifled: women's voices, voices of color, voices of persons with diabilities, gay and lesbian voices, other marginalized voices. We the church are called to release people's gifts, not stifle them.

Next Jesus says some words that have been misinterpreted:

"For you always have the poor with you." (14:7)

Some people use these words to justify a callous disregard for the poor: "You can't do anything for the poor; they'll always be around." This phrasing has become a proverb that contradicts Jesus' intent.

Jesus meant the opposite, so he added,

"And you can show kindness to them whenever you wish." (14:7)

He was citing Deuteronomy 15:11 (RSV): "For the poor will never cease out of the land; therefore I command you, You shall open wide your hand . . . to the needy and to the poor, in the land." The church is called by Jesus to treasure the lives of the poor—as they treasure the life of Jesus who waits for us in them.

Jesus then concluded,

"But you will not always have me. She has done what she could; she has anointed my body beforehand for burying." (14:7-8, RSV)

Now the passion of Christ comes back into focus. The woman was acknowledging what the disciples were slow to grasp and slower to accept: that Jesus was on his way to die. Hers was a prophetic act, anointing him for what was to come. (That she anointed his head may also have been a prophetic action, a sign that she was anointing him King, the suffering King of the reign of God.) And the ointment was poured out in an extravagant act of devotion.

The words of Isaac Watts's hymn "When I Survey the Wondrous Cross" express the kind of extravagant love our Lord deserves:

Were the whole realm of nature mine,
That were a present far too small;

Love so amazing, so divine,
Demands my soul, my life, my all.

Bach composed the *St. Matthew Passion* and Francis of
Assisi left his life of ease to serve Jesus in the poor. So poems
have been written, widows given their mites, and cathedrals
have been built. So we modify our lifestyles to support the
work of the kingdom of God in our midst.

The woman who anointed Jesus shows how deep our love
of Christ can be, and Jesus concludes with these words:

"Truly I say to you, wherever the good news is proclaimed
in the whole world, what she has done will be told in re-
membrance of her." (14:9)

As in this chapter, written two millennia after her act!

Every Gift Counts

As this story is set as a parenthesis between acts of treachery
and betrayal, so we live in such a world, with tragedy and evil
all around. It is easy to grow cynical and to court despair. And
yet in the midst of this dark world, we, too, are given the gift
of wonder and the opportunity for beautiful acts of devotion.
Such acts are the heartbeat of the world.

When I was helping the church at Broadway Baptist
raise the money for its new organ, I stood one Sunday to
announce the total pledges to date. As I announced the
figure, I was tempted to round off the number but didn't.
"We have raised," I said, "$1,994,840.17." After worship a
young boy pulled on my robe and said, "That was my seven-
teen cents!" I was so glad I didn't round it off. God doesn't
round it off. Every gift given in love counts.

A number of years ago, I visited a museum in San Francisco where Buddhist wall paintings were on display. In the

last room of the exhibit, I saw a beautiful mandala—six feet across—the design of which was created by thousands of grains of colored sand.

Buddhist monks had traveled from Asia and spent weeks creating this sacred masterpiece. I learned, to my surprise, that when the exhibit was over, they would return to the United States and, in a sacred ceremony, pour the sand out. Just pour it out! Why the "waste"?

A choir practices for hours every week to offer an anthem to God and to the congregation in Sunday worship. The notes ring out into the air and then are gone. But are they really gone? Why the "waste"? Jesus smiles.

NOTES

1. Tell the story of the anointing. Gather with family and friends. Share stories of who has loved you lavishly—a parent, spouse, teacher, coach, or best friend. Then reflect on Jesus' lavish love of us, the one who loving us, loved us to the end. I led such an observance with friends, and it evoked some holy moments.

2. Edith Wyschogrod, in *Saints and Postmodernism*, wrote, "Altruism is intrinsically excessive, the sumptuary expenditure of the life of the discontinuous individual. . . . The saint is an extreme sumptuary, a subject that spends more than she/he has to the point of expending her/his own substance" (Chicago: University of Chicago Press, 1990), 146–47.

3. Robinson Jeffers, "The Excesses of God," *Be Angry at the Sun* (Random House, 1941), as cited in *The Questing Spirit: Religion in the Literature of Our Time* (New York: Coward McCann, 1947), 293.53.

4. Evelyn Underhill, *Worship* (London: Nisbet, 1937), 47–48.

5. C. S. Lewis, in a letter to a friend, as cited in Gail Godwin, *Heart* (New York: HarperCollins, 2001), 175.

6. Ulrich Luz, *Matthew 21–28* (Minneapolis: Fortress, 2005), 337.

7. Albert Camus in *Return to Tipasa*. An internet search will yield a number of translations and variations.

8. See (among other articles) "The NYC That Never Was: The Half-Finished St. John the Divine" https://untappedcities.com/2013/08/29/the-nyc-that-never-was-st-john-the-divine/, accessed November 7, 2018.

9. Parker Palmer, *The Active Life: A Spirituality of Work, Creativity, and Caring* (San Francisco: Jossey-Bass, 1999), 8.

Afterword

After hearing these stories, we can say with Martin Buber, "All real living is meeting. . . . In the beginning is relation."[1]

What would our records of Jesus mean if they contained just his teachings and not his encounters with people? It would be like the Word becoming words rather than the Word becoming flesh. I hope these encounters have become for you fresh encounters with Christ, "tents of meeting" with God, "thin places."

Where have you found yourself in these stories so they call up your own sacred stories?

Nicodemus met Jesus by night, and Jesus offered him the mystery of new birth. We aren't told in John 3 how the man responded, but we know that at some point he answered yes and helped Joseph of Arimathea provide a holy burial for Jesus. How has the Spirit brought new birth to you? Has it happened all at once or over time?

Jesus met the Samaritan woman and offered "living water" that wells up to eternal life. They carried on a serious theological conversation; then he sent her to be an apostle to her Samaritan village. How have you experienced that living water deep within, welling up to eternal life? Does Jesus' crossing racial, gender, and religious barriers to bring the woman eternal life stir you and give you hope?

Jesus met the paralyzed man by the pool and asked him, "Do you want to be healed?" Sometimes we are not ready yet to be healed, ready to do what it takes to be healed. And yet, he still asks us all that question.

Jesus met the Canaanite woman who came to him for the healing of her daughter. Trusting in a deeper yes than all the noes she had experienced, she matched wits with Jesus, who then changed his mind and healed her daughter. Who do you know who has such a passionate and tenacious faith?

A woman who had been taken in adultery was dragged before Jesus. Jesus shielded her and forgave her and gave her a new life. Where has Jesus shielded you from the condemners of your life? When has his forgiveness set you free?

Jesus healed a woman bent over for eighteen years. How has life bent you over? Where have you been crushed in spirit? Do you know the kind of joy this woman must have felt when she was healed?

Jesus met two wealthy men, the rich young ruler and Zacchaeus the tax collector. The stories call us to examine our relationship with wealth. "Go, sell what you own, and give the money to the poor, and you will have treasure in heaven; then come, follow me," he commanded the rich young ruler. In what ways are you selling and giving? The rich young ruler said no to Jesus, and Zacchaeus said yes. How are you saying no and saying yes to Jesus?

Jesus took two tries to heal a man's eyes in a miracle of two stages. Sometimes healing takes time on our journey toward wholeness. How has this ongoing healing happened to you?

Jesus stopped and heard the cry of blind Bartimaeus. The disciples went to the man and said, "Rise, take heart, he is calling you!" Jesus asked, "What do you want me to do for you?" What would you say if Jesus asked you that question? How would your church answer? How are you and your church saying to the world, "Take heart; get up, he is calling you"? Who is this Jesus you are introducing to them? Does this chapter feel like good news, *euangelion*, to you?

A woman pours a whole container of expensive perfume over Jesus, proclaiming him King and anointing him beforehand for burial. How she must have loved him! What extravagant gift of yourself have you offered, or might you offer to Jesus and the world God so loved?

Who is this Man who brings you new birth and living water, and crosses all kinds of boundaries to do so? Who is this Man who heals and forgives, and stirs up faith and is willing to change his mind in conversation with a feisty Canaanite woman? Who is this Man who defends the sinner and forgives with God's own forgiveness? Who calls us to freedom and from our own sick attachment to things? Who is he whose way of compassion is itself a way of healing?

He is Jesus, who meets us exactly as we are, who takes our hand and leads us to a newer, truer life. He is Jesus the Christ, who is, to use the words of George Buttrick, "surprise of Mercy, outgoing gladness, Rescue, Healing and Life."[2] He is the one from God who comes to meet us and bring us home to God, to self, and to life itself. Living is in the meeting.

NOTES

1. Martin Buber, *I and Thou* (New York: Scribner, 1958), 11, 18.

2. George A. Buttrick, *Prayer* (New York: Abingdon, 1942), 83.

Discussion Guide

Chapter 1: Jesus and Nicodemus

1. Did you grow up hearing stories of your own birth? How did those stories or the absence of those stories shape your sense of self and your connections with others?

2. In what context did you first hear the phrase "born again"? What thoughts or feelings did that phrase prompt in you then? What thoughts and feelings does it prompt now?

3. Do you have a "conversion story"? How has that story or its absence affected your spiritual life?

4. What sort of experiences have led to spiritual beginnings or awakenings in your own life? How is that like or unlike a "conversion story" or "testimony"?

5. Why do you think Nicodemus believed that Jesus had come from God? What do you think he hoped for when he came to Jesus?

6. Does your religious circle encourage curiosity? Are there questions you are afraid to ask in your church because you fear disapproval?

7. The author says, "A God without mystery is an idol." What other things can become idols when they are stripped of their mystery?

8. Think about the times when you've had to begin again. What persuaded you that a restart was necessary? What gave you the courage to begin again?

9. You may have heard the saying, "In the beginner's mind there are many possibilities; in the mind of the expert there are but a few." In what ways was Jesus asking Nicodemus to exchange his expert's mind for the mind of a beginner? What might it mean for you to adopt a beginner's mind?

10. Once-born or twice-born: how aptly do these terms describe your own spiritual experience? Have you been a part of a religious tradition that valued one over the other? What effect did that have on how you valued your own story?

11. Whether you are "once-born," "twice-born," or "many-born," how have you experienced your "utter belovedness"?

12. What sort of new beginning might Jesus be inviting you to hope for?

Chapter 2: Jesus and the Samaritan Woman

1. What's the longest amount of time you've gone without clean running water?

2. When have you been really thirsty? What was it like to be able to drink again?

3. Race, class, gender, education, geography: what are some of the prejudices that have had an effect on your life?

4. This woman could have given Jesus a drink silently. Why do you think she started a conversation? If you could ask Jesus a conversation-starting question, what would it be?

5. What do you think of Jesus' continuing a conversation with this woman without judging or correcting her morals or living situation?

6. What does the phrase "living water" mean to you?

7. Have you ever been offered acceptance and encouragement from an unexpected source? How hard was it to accept? What happened as a result?

8. Who are the ancestors you revere? What might it mean for Jesus to be greater than they?

9. When have you found yourself changed by a theological or spiritual conversation?

10. Nicodemus encountered Jesus in the night, and this woman encountered Jesus at noon. Whether indoors, outdoors, alone, in church, with words or in silence, where and how have you felt a deep connection with God?

11. Many churches are tangled in what some call "worship wars": passionate disagreement over styles and purposes of worship. What does it mean to you and your church to "worship in spirit and in truth"?

12. In your familial and religious traditions, what is the proper role for women, and are women allowed to carry as much spiritual authority as men? What would change in the leadership of your family and church if women and men were considered equal?

13. What cultural, racial, national, gender, and religious lines need to be crossed before God's plan of universal salvation can become a reality?

14. What would change for you if the author's words, "You are my beloved. Live in my love. You are my apostle. Spread that love. It is saving the world," became the underground music of your life?

Chapter 3: Jesus and the Man by the Pool

1. In this chapter, Jesus comes where there were many in need of healing. How easy or difficult is it for you to go to hospitals, nursing homes, or other places where you are in the company of the sick or disabled?

2. Have you ever drawn back from an opportunity to be made more healthy? What do you think was behind your reluctance?

3. What does wholeness mean to you? In what ways have you seen a long-term illness or disability alter a person's identity?

4. The author says that your needs are holy to God. In what ways are you reluctant to admit your own needs? How often do you think you hide your needs so that you don't appear "needy"?

5. To whom can you safely speak about unmet needs and unhealed wounds?

6. In your opinion, what sort of people deserve to be healed? Jesus doesn't place moral requirements on anyone before he heals them; what are your thoughts about that?

7. How do you and how does your faith community approach the idea of Jesus as a healer?

8. In this chapter the author reveals some of his own wounds. How comfortable or uncomfortable are you with spiritual leaders who reveal their own struggles with health and wholeness?

9. If wholeness is a journey, in what ways are you still a beginner on that journey?

10. In some, woundedness leads to compassion, while in others it leads to bitterness. What do you think makes the difference?

11. What is your longest-held hope for your own healing and wholeness? Is it possible to be spiritually whole and remain unhealed?

12. What changes in your own life would bring healing and wholeness closer to you?

13. How can you and your faith community carry on Jesus' ministry of healing to each other and to the hurting world around you?

Chapter 4: Jesus and the Canaanite Woman

1. Tell a story about a time when you followed your first impulse and later regretted it, or a story about a time when you changed your mind and were later glad you did.

2. Where do you go and what do you do to give your mind and soul a rest?

3. Have you ever been asked to do something that was not your job? What did you do?

4. In your spiritual experience, when has tradition been a help, and when has it been an obstacle?

5. It's been said that "I need help" is a sentence that leads to wisdom. How desperate do you have to be to ask for help, and why do you think that it's so hard?

6. The author uses the words *tenacious*, *passionate*, and *persistent* to describe this woman's faith. When have you seen faith like this in others and in yourself?

7. In your religious tradition, how loud, demanding, needy, or persistent can a woman become before she is considered to be out of line?

8. This woman was fighting for the life of her daughter, but to the disciples she was a loud nuisance. How do you see people replaying this same lack of understanding today, and what can be done about it?

9. What sort of person would feel like an outsider in your faith community?

10. Do you set boundaries on whom or what you will give yourself to? What are the guidelines you use for doing that?

11. When was the last time you felt really ignored? Have you ever felt that your prayers were ignored by God? How did you respond?

12. The author says that this woman's concern for her daughter became its own kind of faith. When has your passion for the welfare of others become a kind of faith?

13. What do you think it was that surprised and impressed Jesus about this woman's response to him?

14. This woman seems to have believed that Jesus' leftovers were all her daughter needed. What do you think this says about the kind of faith that delights God?

15. How in your own faith journey have you wrestled with Scripture, with God, or with what your religion told you about God? What did you receive as a result of that struggle?

16. The author writes in this chapter that as a result of faith, Jesus changed his mind. How does it encourage or unsettle you to think that God and Jesus are capable of change?

Chapter 5: Jesus and the Woman Taken in Adultery

1. What's the most embarrassing thing to ever happen to you in public? Have you ever had a nightmare about being naked in public?

2. Why do you think this passage is rarely read as part of Sunday morning worship? What would some congregations find difficult about this passage? Why do you think this passage may have been more important to the early church than it is to the church today?

3. Have you heard this passage taught or preached in worship? What impression did it leave with you?

4. What sort of people or people groups are your political or religious communities most likely to view with contempt?

5. What's the difference between practicing wise discernment and judging people?

6. In what ways was this a trap set for the woman, and in what ways was it a trap set for Jesus?

7. A sexually promiscuous woman was a chief sinner in Jesus' culture. Who are the chief sinners in our culture?

8. In what ways do we elevate sexual sins above all other sins? How would a known adulterer be treated in your church or workplace?

9. This woman was facing a death penalty for her sin. What do you and your faith community think about capital punishment? What sins and crimes, if any, do you think deserve the death penalty?

10. The author imagines Jesus shielding the woman from harm with his own body. How do you find yourself reacting to that image?

11. Why do you think the eldest in the crowd left first? If you were in the crowd, when do you think you would have left? When has Jesus taken the stone out of your hand and kept you from judgment?

12. Have you ever felt yourself the object of shame and humiliation? How did you deal with that? What words and actions by others make that shame better or worse?

13. What is the purpose of shame? Are there amounts of shame that are healthy? How would your life and relationships change if you believed God did not want you to live in shame?

14. How did the lack of accusation from Jesus give the woman in this story a new start and a new future? What kind of future might Jesus want to give to you?

Chapter 6: Jesus and the Bent-Over Woman

1. If Jesus appointed you supervisor of his kingdom, what would you do first?

2. When has laughter been healing for you?

3. Have you ever had to deal with trauma, chronic pain, or long-term illness? How did it shape you mentally and emotionally?

4. Depression, poverty, chronic illness, an inability to "just get over it," a lack of what culture defines as beauty: if you've experienced these, have they been a cause of feeling blamed or shamed?

5. In your life, is it more difficult to bear your own suffering or the suffering of a loved one?

6. The author speaks of being bent over in spirit and crushed in heart. Have you endured times that could be described that way?

7. What are your beliefs and what has your faith tradition taught you about Satan? How does thinking of Satan as "the voice of accusation" fit with your beliefs?

8. In your own life, when and from whom have you suffered extreme criticism? Currently, how loud is the voice of your own inner critic?

9. Jesus took the initiative to heal this woman without asking her about her faith. Why do you think he did that, and why might it matter?

10. When have you experienced the grace and compassion of what the author calls the church beneath the church?

11. In what ways have you experienced the church as a community of judgers or of praisers? How do you think people and churches move from a judging spirit to a praising spirit?

12. When have you experienced the sense of purity and peace that Frederick Buechner found in the Chapel of Saint John? When have you felt yourself to be in the dungeon of "Little Ease"?

13. What is it that most often keeps you from living exuberantly or self-compassionately?

14. When you look back on times of trauma in your life, how was God a partner with you on the path to healing?

15. What means has Jesus used to bring you healing and hope in times of pain, and how do you think Jesus has used you to pass that healing and hope along to others?

Chapter 7: Jesus and the Rich Young Ruler and Zacchaeus

1. On a scale from poverty to wealth, where do you perceive yourself to be? What would you do if you suddenly became very wealthy?

2. The story of the rich young ruler was included by the early church in three Gospels. Why do you think this story was so important to them? Why do you think our relationship to money was so important to Jesus?

3. What is it that worries you most about money, and why do you think money is so hard to talk about?

4. What does your faith tradition teach about eternal life and how to attain it? What does "eternal life" mean to you? What does it mean to have "treasure in heaven"?

5. The rich young ruler seems to have worked his whole life to avoid doing wrong. How is this different from working to do what is right?

6. "Go, sell, give, and follow": what is frightening about these commands? Which one do you think is the most difficult?

7. Have you heard differing interpretations of Jesus' words, "It is easier for a camel to pass through the eye of a needle than for a rich man to enter heaven"? How did those different interpretations affect your response?

8. In some religious circles financial wealth is a certain sign of God's blessing, a blessing we should all seek. Why then does Jesus speak about the spiritual dangers of wealth and ask this man to dispose of it?

9. Do you think of wealth as a blessing? Do you think of poverty as a curse? What does your faith tradition teach about poverty and the acquisition of wealth?

10. Why do you think Zacchaeus was so intent on seeing Jesus? What do you imagine may have happened at supper that prompted his life-changing conversion?

11. If you had been an observer in the crowd, how do you think you would have responded to Zacchaeus's actions that day?

12. The rich young ruler was asked to give away all of his money, yet Jesus approved of Zacchaeus keeping some of his. Why do you think Jesus didn't apply the same standard to both men?

13. What do you think Zacchaeus gained when he gave up his money? What do you think the rich young ruler lost when he kept his?

14. How do these stories inform and challenge you as you consider your relationship to wealth?

15. When has God done something for you that once seemed impossible?

Chapter 8: Jesus and the Blind Man

1. What kind of get-rich, get-well, get-thin-quick schemes have tempted you?

2. What injuries that you've sustained have been slow or fast to heal?

3. In some churches, sickness is considered the result of a lack of faith. What does your faith tradition teach about people who pray for a healing but don't get well?

4. Paul prayed for a healing he never received. What are your thoughts about that? When in your own life have you understood God's strength to have been made perfect in your weakness?

5. When you consider your personal story of a long recovery, what were some of the ways it was "punctuated by healings"?

6. In what ways is the author's distinction between a cure, a healing, and wholeness helpful to you?

7. The author postulates that perhaps we are never completely whole but always on the way toward wholeness. How does that resonate with your own experience?

8. In the face of life's challenges what does it mean to you to "never give in," and how do you balance that with accepting the will of God?

9. What does the word *salvation* mean to you? In what ways is salvation a journey, and in what ways is it a once-in-a-lifetime event? What would change in you if you thought of salvation as a process?

10. The man at the pool had no one to help him, and the man in this story had a village. How much solitude or community do you need when you're facing tough times?

11. In what ways have you experienced spiritual blindness? How has deepening your spiritual understanding changed your life and your relationships?

12. What do you think Jesus was hoping his disciples would see and hear with open eyes and open ears? What do you think Jesus is hoping that you will see and hear?

13. The author speaks of healings that are deeper than physical healings. What is a deep healing you long for?

14. What sort of miracle do you hope may be on the way for you?

Chapter 9: Jesus and Blind Bartimaeus

1. When is life most joyful for you?

2. Have you ever felt shushed, or been told to shut up? What was your response to that?

3. Whose lives in your community matter most and whose matter least? What do you think of protest as a means of achieving equal respect?

4. How open are you and the members of your faith circle to acknowledging yourselves as sinners?

5. What do you think people are trying to protect themselves from when they look away from those in need?

6. How do you tell the difference between a wish, a want, and a deep need?

7. Paul says that he has in all things learned to be content (Philippians 4:12), and advises contentment (1 Timothy 6:6), yet Bartimaeus yells out his needs and Jesus heals him. When and how do you think it's appropriate to express an unmet need? What do you think God thinks you should do about unmet needs?

8. When have you experienced a holy interruption? What happened, and what did you do about it?

9. In your mind, does the word *evangelical* describe a person's faith, or describe a person's politics? What are your thoughts about the changing social perceptions of the term "evangelical"?

10. Have you ever been urged by your church to evangelize others? How do you respond to the word *evangelism* now? What's the good news in the gospel you proclaim?

11. When have you experienced the gospel as a series of noes? How does it make you feel to think that God's word to us in Jesus is not yes and no, but yes?

12. When and how have you recently experienced the gladness of the good news of the gospel?

13. How might the message of God's unconditional love shape your spiritual life? When do you find yourself doubting that God's love is unconditional?

14. What helps you when you are trying to hear Christ's voice and love it: music, art, worship, nature, reading, or something else?

15. In what ways might Jesus be calling for you today? In what ways would he like you to bring closer to him someone else whom he is calling?

Chapter 10: Jesus and the Woman Who Anointed Him at Bethany

1. When have you followed a generous impulse and been glad you did?

2. Where and how have you found an interlude of peace during a stressful time?

3. Where do you go to see God going beyond the necessary to give us something beautiful in this world?

4. How does your faith community observe Holy Week? How might an anointing service at a home or in church enhance the week?

5. When have you experienced what the author calls the extravagant kindness of God?

6. Who in your life has given generously to you without expecting return?

7. How does Jesus' death move you by its sacrifice?

8. When have you sacrificed so that you could offer something to God and for God's work in the world?

9. How does your church find a balance between making worship beautiful and caring for the poor?

10. Which is harder for you: giving generously or receiving graciously?

11. What are some of the ways you express your own adoration of Christ?

12. Have you ever felt misunderstood because of the ways you sought to follow Jesus? Describe that experience.

13. In your faith circles, whose voices are most prized and whose gifts are most elevated? Whose gifts and voices are most likely to be ignored?

14. How and for what would you like to be remembered?

Afterword

1. The author quotes Martin Buber, "All real living is meeting." What are a few of the encounters that have been most influential in your own life?

2. As you've read these stories of the encounters that others had with Jesus, how have your own impressions of him changed?

3. Where in the stories of these encounters have you found characters that you've identified with?

4. If you've been reading these stories with a group, how has encountering Jesus together changed your relationships with each other?